Dear Bob,

I wish you PEACE
HEALTH & HAPPINESS!
Your FRIENDSHIP
IS ONE OF MY
MOST CHERISHED GIFTS!

Koren

Basic Prevention

A Guide to Healthy Aging

By

Francis A. Salerno, MD with Henry A. Acres

Illustrations by Kathy Moser

authorHOUSE®

AuthorHouse™
1663 Liberty Drive, Suite 200
Bloomington, IN 47403
www.authorhouse.com
Phone: 1-800-839-8640

AuthorHouse™ UK Ltd.
500 Avebury Boulevard
Central Milton Keynes, MK9 2BE
www.authorhouse.co.uk
Phone: 08001974150

First published by AuthorHouse   6/2/2008

ISBN: 978-1-4343-3477-0 (sc)

Library of Congress Control Number: 2007906444

Printed in the United States of America
Bloomington, Indiana

This book is printed on acid-free paper.

May 2008

We have worked hard and long to make this book as helpful as possible to people who want to age successfully. Our work, however, could not have occurred without the support, direct and indirect, from many people. And so we give thanks here to our many colleagues in the medical and academic communities whose high standards and desire to learn have guided us. We thank the thousands of patients Fran has served at the Reading and Lehigh Valley Hospitals and the thousands of students Henry has seen at The Institute for Learning in Retirement; they have reminded us that each person is special and important.

On her own time, Kathy Robinson guided the project from a few pages of notes to a finished book. Thanks, Kathy.

And finally, we thank Aleita Salerno and Irene Acres for their unflagging encouragement, support—and patience. This book is dedicated to them.

Fran Salerno
Henry Acres

Aging is not a disease; it's a normal part of life. BASIC PREVENTION is your guide to aging successfully. It will help you increase the time in your older years when you are independent and enjoying your life. It may decrease the time, if any, in your older years when you must depend on others to help you through the day.

Each section of BASIC PREVENTION concludes with "What You Can Do." Find out what you can do to keep your mind sharp, to keep your bones strong, to avoid falls, to understand what cholesterol is, to understand what medicines you should — and should not — take, to understand what your blood pressure tells you, and to learn many other things that will help you age successfully.

The second part of BASIC PREVENTION is titled COMMON PROBLEMS. Here you will learn what you need to know about back pain, constipation, dementia, and other health problems that are common among older people.

If you are in your 30's, 40's, 50's, or 60's, BASIC PREVENTION can help your older years be healthy ones. If you are in your 70's or 80's, BASIC PREVENTION can make your present years more enjoyable.

You have only one body, one life. Let BASIC PREVENTION show you how to take charge now and increase your chances of enjoying your older years.

Table of Contents

Basic Prevention

Introduction

Hello. I'm Fran Salerno. As a geriatrician—that is, a doctor who specializes in treating older people—I deeply enjoy the art, the science and the practice of medicine. My patients have taught me a great deal about aging, and I want you to benefit from what they have taught me.

Simply put, you cannot stop the aging process. But you can learn how to age successfully— that is to increase the time when you are "young old" and enjoying life, and decrease the time when you may become "frail old" and no longer able to function independently.

This introduction has six sections:

- THE NORMAL AGING PROCESS: WHAT WE CAN ALL EXPECT

- THE DIFFERENCE BETWEEN DISEASE AND ILLNESS

- CHRONIC DISEASES THAT AFFLICT OLDER PEOPLE

- THE HEALTH CARE SYSTEM: HOW IT WORKS.

- PREVENTIVE CARE: PHYSICAL, PSYCHOLOGICAL, SOCIAL AND SPIRITUAL

- BASIC PREVENTION: WHAT YOU CAN DO.

---

1. THE NORMAL AGING PROCESS: WHAT WE CAN ALL EXPECT

Aging is not a disease. It is a series of normal changes in our bodies. In and of themselves, these changes may slow us down somewhat, but they do not result in significant harmful effects.

Here's what to expect as you grow old:

Decreases in ...

light that reaches the retina

blood flow to/through the brain

blood flow to the kidney

blood flow to the liver

brain mass

cardiac heart function

function of the liver

kidney function

hearing

height

lung function

maximum heart rate

muscle mass

reaction time

taste buds sensitivity

body water

vision

Increases in...

fat mass

prostate gland (doubles in size)

These normal changes do not seriously impair the way we function. They are not considered diseases. Again, they are *normal.*

2. THE DIFFERENCE BETWEEN DISEASE AND ILLNESS

A disease is a process. Illness is the body's subjective response to a disease.

For example, hypertension is a disease that can result in the illness of a heart attack or stroke. Many people with hypertension lead normal lives. In short, we can have a disease and still function normally. But when a disease brings on an illness, the result is functional decline and frailty.

Causes of Death:

- Acute onset with fatal outcome in 1-3 years. (e.g., heart disease, cancer.) Accounts for about 20% of US deaths.
- Chronic diseases with fatal outcomes in 3-7 years. (e.g., pulmonary disease, kidney failure, congestive heart failure.) Accounts for about 20% of US deaths.
- Geriatric syndromes with fatal outcomes in 1-20 years.(e.g. Alzheimer's, arthritis.) These are characterized by frailty and decline in functioning. The health system's reactive model fails to address the psychological, social, spiritual and financial aspects of these diseases. (See COMMON PROBLEMS). Because a cure is not an attainable goal, palliative care, which focuses on relieving the symptoms and understanding the patient's personal life goals (See ADVANCED DIRECTIVES) is the treatment. Accounts for about 40% of US deaths.
- Others that lead to immediate death. (e.g., suicides and accidents.)

Accounts for about 20% of US deaths.

3. CHRONIC DISEASES THAT AFFECT OLDER PEOPLE

Also normal, however, is the fact that as we grow older most of us will have one or more chronic diseases. These are diseases that are not acute but recur and last over a period of time. Frequently occurring chronic diseases include:

- *Osteoarthritis (the wear and tear of joints and the wearing away of joint cartilage)*
- *Rheumatoid arthritis (inflammation of joints with erosion of the bones around the joints)*
- *Hypertension or increased blood pressure*
- *Hearing loss*
- *Chronic, ischemic heart disease (narrowing and blockage of blood vessels in the heart).*
- *Irregular heart rhythms*
- *Congestive heart failure (failure of the heart to work well as a pump)*
- *Chronic sinus problems*
- *Glaucoma (pressure in the eye)*
- *Cataracts*
- *Osteoporosis (thinning of the bones)*
- *Diabetes mellitus (sugar in the blood)*
- *Skin disorders*
- *Abnormality of blood fats, leading to hardening of the arteries, heart attacks, and strokes*

- *Chronic lung diseases*
- *Alcohol overuse*
- *Neurological disorders including Parkinson's Disease and Alzheimer's Dementia*
- *Sleep disorders*

People with some of these diseases lose their ability to function normally; they no longer can do what they'd like to do in the daily activities of their lives. The buildup of multiple diseases leads to multiple visits to a doctor and, often, to multiple doctors. That can lead to multiple medications, which can lead to drug-drug interactions, many of which are harmful.

The calling cards of these diseases are known as the *Geriatric Syndromes.* The Geriatric Syndromes are symptoms of functional decline which, if left unrecognized and untreated, lead to further functional decline and ultimately, death.

Among the common geriatric syndromes are:

- *Falls*
- *Memory Impairment*
- *Acute episodes of confusion*
- *Balance problems and dizziness*
- *Weight loss*
- *Back pain*
- *Constipation*

- *Bowel and urinary incontinence*

These Geriatric Syndromes are the common symptoms doctors deal with daily as they try to get behind the symptom, identify the cause and treat it.

4. THE HEALTH CARE SYSTEM AND OUR AGING POPULATION

Our health care system is, for the most part, reactive; that is, it kicks in when someone is sick or injured. Hospitals came about during the Industrial Revolution as places to treat injured workers. Their wounds were sutured and their fractures treated with casts. Surgical procedures developed as anesthesia became sophisticated.

Those beginnings gave the current health care system these characteristics:

- *Acute-care oriented*
- *Hospital oriented*
- *Sub-specialty oriented*
- *Little, if any, emphasis on preventive care.*

Until recently, insurance companies did not reimburse patients or doctors for *well visits* (e.g., for routine exams and checkups). We have a pretty good system to help us when we are sick or injured. Unfortunately, that system doesn't do much to help us from becoming sick and injured. This has special meaning for the aging and the still-well population.

U.S. Population Data:

YEAR	POPULATION OVER AGE 65
1900	4%
2002	13 – 14%
2040	25% (projected)

At present, about 1% of Americans are over 85 (almost 3 million people). This is the group that has multiple chronic diseases and, as result, is the greatest per capita consumer of health care dollars.

This situation is of great concern to health care financial planners. By 2040, 5%, or one out of 20, will be over 85 and living with multiple chronic diseases. The question that looms is: Can our current health care system meet the challenges of the increasing population of older adults?

The answer is "No."

If our system must develop preventive care programs for the aging but still well population, these programs must recognize psychological and social needs, as well as physical ones. We will not meet the challenges of an aging population if our health care system continues to focus on the reactive model of care.

The time line shown here illustrates how health care is delivered by age. We get a lot of attention when we are babies and children. We don't get much from our teens to our middle years. At around 50, we start getting more care and at age 65 and beyond we use a great portion of the health care system's resources.

<pre>
/////////   /////   ///   /////   ///////   ///////////////
Birth to 5   5 – 15   15 – 50   50 – 65   65 – 75   75+
</pre>

Good care of older adults does not begin at 65 or 75. Good care for all of us begins at birth, continues through childhood, and *should* (but does not) continue throughout our lives.

Good infant and childhood care, immunizations, antibiotics, medical technologies and public health interventions have increased life expectancy in this country from 44 years in 1900 to 76 years in 2000.

But we have new challenges. We are much more inactive than we used to be because of computer use and the entertainment industry. One result is obesity, a condition that leads to bad outcomes and an increase in diabetes mellitus and heart disease, among others.

5.   PREVENTIVE   CARE: PHYSICAL,

PSYCHOLOGICAL, AND SOCIAL

Each of us has psychological and social needs that affect our health, and it is especially important that we recognize these needs in older people. The preventive care strategies set out by the United States Preventive Care Task Force and the Canadian Task Force on Preventive Care do not include psychological and social needs. But these needs affect the health of all of us and are especially important for older people.

Where you live, with whom you live, and your financial picture are determining factors in how healthy you will be in your later years.

Older people share many common concerns, among them:

- *Affordable Housing*
- *Long-Term Care (What is it? Who can deliver it? What is the role/status of direct caregivers?)*
- *Transportation*
- *The Security of Social Security*
- *Will Medicare Continue?*
- *The Cost of Medications*
- *The Side Effects of Multiple Medications*
- *Loneliness/Isolation*
- *The decreasing number of doctors able/willing to provide care exclusively to older people*

These are issues we must include as part of preventive care. John Donne wrote, "No man is an island." How true that is! The current health care system does not and cannot meet the needs of older adults. Medicare alone cannot meet these needs. Our communities must partner with the health system and the federal government to redefine a system of ongoing care. No one should be an island.

6. BASIC PREVENTION: WHAT YOU CAN DO

BASIC PREVENTION offers strategies that may help you increase the time of your life when you are well and decrease the time when you may be frail and sick. I have blended information in the United States Preventive Care Task Force Report with recommendations that are intuitive and directed at older adults' psychosocial needs.

Some of this information is based on my observations of people who seem to age successfully—men and women who continue living a full, active life with a sense of integrity and self-worth for a longer span of years.

This information is represented by the acronym BASIC PREVENTION.

Each letter of these two words represents one or more preventive care strategies. If you follow these, you will be taking some responsibility for your own care and health as you age. By all means, discuss these strategies with your doctor.

Best wishes to you as you go from B is for Brain to N is for Neoplasm, and do what you can to age successfully!

It's Your Brain - Protect It

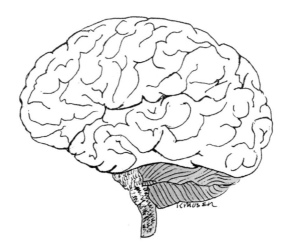

Brain

B is for
Brain Health

It is fitting that the chapter on brain health is the first topic I present in this book. In one way or another every chapter that follows contributes to the maintenance of your brain. In medical school, one of my favorite mentors called the brain "Numero Uno." Through the brain, we conceive, plan and carry out the very simple to the most complex tasks that are essential for our physical, psychological and social well-being. All of the body's organs serve the brain. They are also controlled by the brain. For example, sight, hearing, touch, smell and taste are the connections between the brain and the outside world.

The brain controls our temperature, our heart rate and our blood pressure. The heart delivers 70% of the volume of blood with each heartbeat to the brain in order to provide it with essential nutrients and oxygen. Certain areas of the brain enable us to have coordinated movements such as walking, playing a violin, driving a motor vehicle and eating a pizza. The brain tells us when we are thirsty and hungry. When we eat we are supplying energy the brain needs to continue to function. The history of science suggests that the brain has evolved over millions of years. Early life forms essentially consisted of a simple organism with a mouth, a GI tract and the ability to eliminate waste. There were no eyes or ears, no arms or legs. Over the past 10 million years the human species has evolved complete with vision, hearing, taste, smell and touch. It also has evolved into the ability to receive and process information, create memories and think. We can recall events from the past, live in the present and dream about the future. No wonder my mentor called the brain Numero Uno.

The brain is a miracle. It weighs about three pounds and is the size of a medium cauliflower. It is divided into two half spheres called hemispheres. Each sphere is divided into sections called lobes, each of which serves a particular purpose. In the rear of the brain, the left occipital lobe is responsible for sight, and the right occipital lobe is responsible for hearing. Some lobes store memories, while others are responsible for behavior.

Many older adults fear a loss of brain power that can lead to reduced memory and one of the dementia illnesses such as Alzheimer's Disease. For the rest of this chapter I will focus on what we can normally expect as we and our brains age. Does this sound familiar? "My memory isn't what it used to be. I must be getting older." It should. Tens of thousands of older adults say it every day. Are the people who say this in a state of mental decline? Are they losing *cognitive vitality?*

Cognitive vitality refers to a number of thinking skills, such as how well we can pay attention, learn new things, remember, use language, follow procedures and make decisions. It is a measure of how well our brains work.

Remember these two things: First, although some cognitive decline is fairly common in later life, **it is not an inevitable part of aging.** Many elderly people, including ones in their 90s and 100s, maintain cognitive vitality; in simple terms, they remain "sharp."

Second, recent research shows that certain prevention practices can help us achieve and maintain cognitive vitality in late life.

As we reach the later stages of our lives, each of us will be at one of these levels of cognitive vitality:

- **Full Cognitive Vitality.** This is the smallest group. People in it have the same strong mental skills they had throughout their adult lives.

- **AAMI (Age-Associated Memory Impairment).** People in this group may complain of occasional memory lapses that occur as a normal part of aging. But they function normally and, compared to their age groups, have normal scores on brain performance tests. Most people with AAMI *will not* develop further cognitive impairment

- **MCI (Mild Cognitive Impairment).** People in this group complain of memory loss. Compared

17

to their age groups, they score below normal on brain performance tests. People with MCI function normally and maintain normal levels of other cognitive skills such as language and abstract thinking. However, their situation may deteriorate. Some 15% of people with MCI develop dementia each year and 50% will develop dementia within three years of diagnosis.

- **Dementia.** Chronic, progressive and irreversible, dementia destroys the brain's capacity to function normally. Dementia is common in old age: up to 25% of people over 75 and 40% of people over 80 have some form of dementia. The most common forms are Alzheimer's Disease and vascular dementia. (See *Common Problems – Dementia*).

In conclusion, most of us will have some cognitive impairment in our later years. The majority will be in the Age Associated Memory Impairment group (AAMI). We'll have occasional memory lapses but will function normally and have normal age-group scores on brain performance tests.

Others will be in the Mild Cognitive Impairment group (MCI). These people will function normally but will score below average for their age group on brain performance tests.

Some of us will decline into a form of dementia, the most common of which is Alzheimer's Disease (AD).

WHAT YOU CAN DO

Early detection: Early detection of cognitive impairment can result in treatment programs to control the difficulty. At present, various approaches, including brain performance testing, brain imaging, biomarkers and genetic markers, are used to detect early stages of MCI or dementia.

Lifestyle Management: Create some "Brain Reserves" that will maintain a healthy level of cognitive vitality:

- Be socially active. Speaking with other people and participating in group activities will stimulate your cognitive capacities. As exercise strengthens your body, social interaction strengthens your mind. *Avoid isolation. Be with others!*

- Do things that require some intellectual work. Remaining in the work force part-time or working as a volunteer will help to keep your mind active (and also provide social interaction).

- Engage in lifelong learning. Take a course, join a book club.

- Exercise regularly. (See *E is for Exercise.*)

- Eat properly. (See *N is for Nutrition — how and what we eat.*)

Treat any diseases you may have: Many conditions, especially those considered risk factors for cardiovascular disease, are also risk factors for cognitive decline with aging and dementia. These conditions include:

- Hypertension. (See *P is for Pressure.*)
- Diabetes. (See *Common Problems – Obesity.*)
- Excessive Cholesterol. (See *C is for Cholesterol.*)
- Depression. (See *Common Problems – Depression.*)
- Adverse Drug Reactions. (See *R is for Rx (Medications.*)
- Substance Abuse — (tobacco, alcohol and illicit drugs. (See *V is for Vices.*)

Your brain is a magnificent organ. To keep it healthy, **USE IT!!!**

Do I Have A Bone
To Pick With You

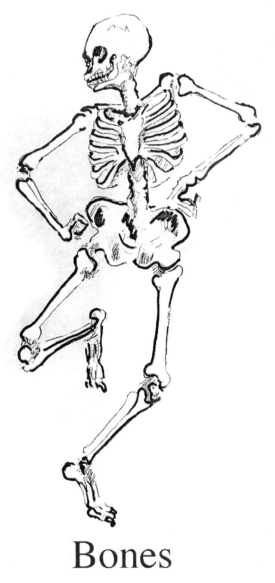

Bones

B is for

Bones

When you think Osteoporosis, you probably think "milk." You're right, but there's more. Read on.

Osteo means bone. *Porosis* means porous. Put them together and you get *Osteoporosis*, a medical term that describes the condition of having porous and thin bones.

You probably know osteoporosis as the condition that results in easily broken bones, a loss in height or a "hump" that grows on the back. Women are especially vulnerable to the disease and its uncomfortable results, but men should also pay close attention. If you can answer "yes" to any of the following questions, you may be at increased risk for osteoporosis:

Are you female, with a small build and a fair complexion?

Are you of oriental descent?

Do you smoke?

Are you currently using a thyroid hormone medication?

Do you take corticosteroids?

Did your mother have osteoporosis?

To help avoid osteoporosis and years of pain that come with it, you should:

- **Take your vitamins:** The National Institute of Health recommends the following guidelines:

Women aged 25 to 50	1000 mg of Calcium daily with Vitamin D
Women Post-Menopausal 50 to 65 on Estrogen Replacement Therapy	1000 mg of Calcium daily with Vitamin D
Women Post-Menopausal 50 to 65 not on Estrogen Replacement Therapy	1500 mg of Calcium daily with Vitamin D
Men aged 25 to 65	1000 mg of Calcium daily with Vitamin D
Men over 65	1500 mg of Calcium daily with Vitamin D

- **Take a walk:** Exercise
- **Give up your smokes:** Understand that tobacco, alcohol and cortisone-based medicines increase your risk of osteoporosis.
- **Take time with your doctor:** Discuss your bone health with your doctor, especially if you have thyroid disease, diabetes or take cortisone- based medicines.

- **Take a test:** Undergo a painless bone densitometry procedure if you are over 60 and want to detect bone loss early.

BONE METABOLISM AND OSTEOPOROSIS

Metabolism is a fancy way to say "change." Bone metabolism simply explains that our bones change throughout our lives. You may want to think of a bone as a storage closet for nutrients like calcium and phosphate which are essential to the heart, muscles and other organs. Bones are in constant change through the processes of *bone formation,* where the bones collect nutrients and are built up, and *bone reabsorption,* where the bones and the nutrients stored in them are broken down. As the storage closet starts to empty, we have to find ways to refill our supply.

When we are young, our bone formation is accelerated as we grow to reach the proper height. Once we reach adult life, the acceleration tapers off and a balance between bone formation and re-absorption is created.

Everyone over the age of 30 begins to lose bone. This process speeds up throughout the 40s, 50s and 60s, especially after menopause in women and andropause in men. The imbalance during these years between bone re-absorption and bone formation results in thinning bones and can lead to osteoporosis. Although found in both sexes, it is more common among women.

When osteoporosis sets in, the bones have become porous and thin. A slight fall can mean a fracture, especially of the hip, spine and other long bones. Slight disfigurement can occur. People with osteoporosis are often bent forward and walk unsteadily. Some women are said to "shrink" as their bones break down in size and they lose height. And some women develop an unpleasant growth known as "Dowagers' Hump" between their shoulders.

You may be among the 50% of people over 65 who have osteoporosis, but you may not yet have experienced its symptoms. To identify the condition quickly and accurately, ask your doctor about a Bone Densitometry test.

DIAGNOSING OSTEOPOROSIS WITH BONE DENSITOMETRY

Physicians today view cholesterol testing as a common procedure to identify people at risk of cardiac diseases. Physicians who specialize in the care of older adults strongly recommend Bone Densitometry in the same light for osteoporosis. By identifying the condition of the bones the procedure far outperforms the basic X-ray.

Bone densitometry is a safe and painless technique that measures bone density at various sites in the back, arms, wrists and hips. The procedure identifies bones that have thinned beyond the point of a normal young adult. Such an outcome indicates osteoporosis and should send you directly to treatment for bone loss. If you are over 65, you should include a densitometry procedure in your next physical.

RISK FACTORS FOR OSTEOPOROSIS

- Decreased levels of hormones in the body that result from the normal aging process
- Chronic use of alcohol and tobacco
- Long-term use of cortisone-type medicines, especially those greater than 7.5 milligrams of Prednisone daily
- High doses of inhaled steroids often used to control asthma symptoms
- High doses of thyroid replacement hormone
- Type 2 Diabetes
- Blood thinning medication to avoid blood clot formation
- Long-term medicinal programs to prevent brain seizures

If you use any of the medicines listed above or if you use alcohol or tobacco regularly, please pursue the bone densitometry. This easy test now can save you a lot of pain in the future.

PREVENTING AND CONTROLLING OSTEOPOROSIS

1. Calcium... Your mother told you to drink your milk. You told your kids to drink their milk. Here's why: 1500 milligrams a day of calcium will enhance bone formation. Your calcium supply comes from milk and dairy products, as well as from spinach and other leafy green vegetables and orange juice. You can also look for calcium supplements in local pharmacies and health food stores.

I strongly recommend that females start using a calcium supplement as teenagers and continue it throughout their lives to build and then maintain strong bones.

2. Vitamin D... Your body needs help putting the calcium to work, and Vitamin D is the right sidekick. Essentially, it helps the stomach wall absorb the calcium. Our bodies manufacture Vitamin D when sunlight hits the skin, but as we age, the skin loses its ability to manufacture the amount of Vitamin D needed to absorb calcium.

You should add a Vitamin D supplement of 800 milligrams daily.

3. Exercise... It's never too late to put on your sneakers. Walking is an effective way to stimulate bone formation, and weight training can provide even more dramatic help. (Although swimming is a healthful exercise, it puts no weight on the bones and thus does nothing to strengthen them.)

I encourage exercise at any age, but recommend a consultation with your primary care physician before starting a program.

4. Treatments ... If you have osteoporosis, other medications are available. These include: Bisphosphonates, such as alendronate (Fosamax) or risedronate (Actonel).

Selective estrogen receptor modulators (SERMs) like Evista can be helpful, too.

(In the past, estrogen was the mainstay of therapy, but it is now associated with many risks including breast cancer, blood clot formation, coronary heart disease, stroke, gallbladder disease and memory impairment. At this time, estrogen therapy (Premarin) is not recommended for osteoporosis.)

SUMMARY OF BONE METABOLISM

At about age 30, we begin an imbalance between bone formation and bone re-absorption, resulting from our natural decrease of estrogen and testosterone. The end result may be thin and brittle bones occurring in both sexes but predominately in women. The resulting osteoporosis increases the risk of fractures of the hip and other long bones and leads to a breakdown of the spine.

WHAT YOU CAN DO

Take your vitamins, (See the chart shown above of recommendations from the National Institute of Health.)

Take a walk: Exercise

Give up your smokes: Understand that tobacco, alcohol and cortisone-based medicines help bring on osteoporosis.

Take time with your doctor: If you are a woman, talk with your doctor about a possible need for estrogen replacement therapy or its alternatives

Take a test: If you are 60 or over, have a painless bone densitometry procedure.

Now you have the tools to avoid and control osteoporosis. Hopefully, you will let them guide you today to the calcium, vitamin D supplements and exercise that will influence bone strength.

Don't Get Burned

Burns

B is also for

Burns

I'll begin this chapter with two facts: First, older people are especially vulnerable to burns. Second, older people who follow the common sense advice given here can greatly reduce that vulnerability.

WHY ARE OLDER PEOPLE VULNERABLE TO BEING BURNED?

For several reasons:

Older people can't move as quickly as they once could. The few extra seconds it may take to move a hand away from a flame, a foot from a burning leaf pile, or a back from a scalding shower can cause a serious burn. The few extra seconds it may take to react to a house fire in the middle of the night can lead to death.

Supportive devices—canes, walkers and wheel chairs-are wonderful aids for people who need them but major hazards when there is a need to get away immediately from a hot surface, an open flame, or a house on fire.

Poor circulation, loss of fatty tissue beneath the skin and nerve tissue degeneration can diminish older people's sense of touch. They may not know that a surface they are touching is really too hot to touch! They may not know that they are getting a bad sunburn!

Trembling hands or reduced manual dexterity can spill a scalding hot cup of tea or coffee and cause a bad burn. (Such burn accidents frequently affect young grandchildren that older people mind.) Memory impairment- which is becoming more common as Alzheimer's and vascular dementia increase exponentially- is a major cause of burns among older people The kitchen, with its hot surfaces, and the bathroom, with the possibility of very hot water, are especially dangerous places for the memory impaired.

SEASONAL WARNINGS!

Winter. In colder climates, people use open fireplaces, kerosene stoves, gas burners, gas and electric ovens to help heat a house or an apartment. Every one of these (and similar heating devices) is an extra hazard for the old.

Additional winter hazards are faulty Christmas lights, especially on indoor trees, poorly vented furnaces, and fireplaces that cause carbon monoxide poisoning.

Spring and Summer. A surprising number of older people are burned when they adjust or just touch an overheated lawnmower. Others get bad cases of sunburn from failing to sense how hot their skin has become.

Fall. Although it is illegal in many locations, many people still burn the piles of leaves they've raked. A significant number of older people burn their hands and legs while doing this.

HOW TO MAKE OLDER PEOPLE LESS VULNERABLE TO BURNS

In the bathroom...

Check your hot water heater to make sure that at its hottest your water does not exceed 120 degrees Fahrenheit. Check the water temperature with your hands. If the water feels too hot to your hand, it *is* too hot. Install anti-scald devices that automatically stop faucet or shower water flow if the temperature is too high.

In the kitchen...

Always keep pot handles turned inward on the stove. Use oven mitts or large potholders. When cooking with grease, have a large lid nearby to cover the pan if a grease fire should start. If one does, cover the pan, turn off the burner, and leave the lid on for at least two hours. Remove the lid carefully. If oxygen reignites the fire, cover the pan again.

If a fire starts in the oven, turn the oven off and keep the door shut until the fire is out.

Avoid loose clothing when cooking. It can ignite easily when you reach from the front to the back burners. Cotton and linen are very flammable. Although synthetic fibers are less flammable, they burn quickly when they do ignite and can melt to the skin. Wool is safest but might be impractical in the kitchen. Though not flame retardant, denim is good. (No flame retardant materials are available for adults.)

Remove throw rugs and other objects that can interfere with canes and walkers. Have a clear, open path between eating and cooking areas.

In and around the house...

Smoke detectors are a must. There should be at least one on each level of the house and one on the ceiling just outside your bedroom door. Test battery operated smoke detectors monthly. Change batteries once a year in all smoke detectors. If there are smokers in the household, have large, safe ashtrays in the areas where people smoke. Have smoke detectors in these areas. Empty ashtrays into metal trash cans

Keep fire escape routes (stairs, hallways) free of clutter. Keep matches and lighters where children can't reach them. Store flammable materials such as paints, paint thinners, solvents, etc., in tightly-shut containers and away from areas where they could ignite. Unplug power tools when not in use.

With electrical appliances, dry your hands before using. Use appliances only on dry surfaces away from water. Unplug them when not in use. Replace appliance cords that are frayed or have brittle insulation.

In case of fire in the house...

Sleep with the bedroom door closed. This puts a barrier between you and a fire. Have an escape plan for everyone in the family and practice it. Have an alternate escape route if the main one is blocked.

If there are a number of people in the house/apartment, have a place outside where you agree to meet to see who is safely out and who is not.

Your bedroom should have a door, a window and a telephone. If you call the fire department, give your location, name, address, phone number and where you (and others) are in the house. Have a flashlight to signal where you are when they arrive.

Stay down. Heat and smoke rise. Crawling will help minimize smoke inhalation and prevent the super hot air from scalding your respiratory system. Get out and **stay out.** Don't go back into a burning building for anything.

What to do when burned...

Drop to the ground and roll to extinguish burning clothing. If you are scalded, immediately remove hot, wet clothing. Use cool water on the burn area immediately to reduce the skin temperature and stop the burning process, to numb the pain and to reduce swelling. After cooling, cover the burn with a clean, dry dressing.

Remove burned clothing, jewelry, tight clothing and boots to cut down on swelling. Keep the victim warm with a cover. Get medical help immediately. Get the victim to a hospital.

DO NOT use ointments, sprays, or butter on a burn

NEVERS...

Never remove a radiator cap from an overheated car.

Never use an elevator in a fire emergency.

Never overload circuits or fuse boxes.

What You Can Do

Remember that although burns are accidents that can happen to anyone at any time, older people are especially vulnerable to these accidents. Follow the advice in this chapter and significantly reduce the possibility of being burned.

Make Your Wishes Known

Advance Directives

A is for

Advance Directives

Imagine that you have a temporary or permanent illness or injury and that there are options regarding the treatment you can receive. You are entitled to make those decisions. But suppose you are unable to make or communicate the decisions you want? An Advance Directive will assure you—and the people closest to you—that your wishes are carried out.

If you don't have an Advance Directive now, PLEASE read this section carefully and then get one. An Advance Directive does two things: it names the person you want to make medical decisions for you when you are unable to speak for yourself, and it explicitly states the kinds of medical treatment you want or do not want.

Five Wishes is one form of an Advance Directive. Sponsored by Aging with Dignity, a non-profit organization. It guides you in making these wishes:

1. *The person I want to make care decisions for me when I can't.*
2. *The kind of medical treatment I want or don't want.*
   (This section includes your wishes regarding Life Support Treatment *Close to Death, In a Coma and*

Not Expected to Wake or Recover, Permanent and Severe Brain Damage, and other conditions.)

3. *My Wish for How Comfortable I Want To Be.*

4. *My Wish for How I Want People To Treat Me.*

5. *My Wish for What I Want My Loved Ones to Know*

You should talk over your wishes with those closest to you: spouse, children and others. When you have signed and witnessed the form, your *Five Wishes* will be legal and valid. Give copies to your doctor, your family, and others who care about you. Keep the original copy in a special place in your home where someone can find it when needed. If you are admitted to a hospital or nursing home, bring a copy of your *Five Wishes* with you and have it placed in your medical record.

Five Wishes or an Advance Directive like it will bring peace of mind to you and those who care for you.

For more information:

1-888-5-WISHES (1-888-594-7437)

Aging With Dignity

PO Box 1661

Tallahassee, Florida 32302-1661

www.agingwith dignity.org

1-888-594-7437.

What You Can Do

BE SURE that you have an Advance Directive.

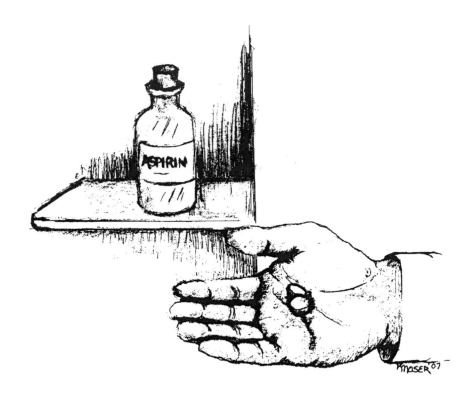

A is also for

Aspirin

Aspirin is truly a wonder drug. Felix Hoffman was a chemist who worked for F. G. Bayer, the German pharmaceutical company. Hoffman's father had severe arthritis. At that time, arthritis was treated with drugs called salicylates, but these had painful side effects. Hoffman worked to develop a drug that would relieve his father's pain while leaving him comfortable. In 1899, after much testing, he developed acetylsalisic acid, which he called aspirin. Because Bayer wanted to be sure the new drug was safe and effective, the company was slow in marketing it. Soon, however, its effectiveness as a pain reliever became known, and today, with billions sold every year, aspirin is the world's most popular drug for pain relief.

Recent studies show that aspirin can be effective in preventing heart attacks, strokes, colon and breast cancer. The American Heart Association recommends aspirin for people who have had a heart attack or stroke.

For the purpose of preventing heart attacks, strokes and colon cancer, we recommend 325 mg of aspirin be taken daily. Aspirin can be life saving for people who are actively having a heart attack. If you are experiencing pain which may be a heart attack, immediately take 325 mg of aspirin and dial 911. Do not drive yourself or have someone drive you. Dialing 911 activates an emergency response system which provides quicker access to health care providers and technology which can save your life.

You should know two basic things about aspirin. First, it can relieve pain and help prevent some major diseases. Second, certain people are allergic to aspirin and may suffer stomach pain, excessive bleeding and bruising from its use. Check with your doctor to see if aspirin is right for you.

What You Can Do

Talk to your doctor about aspirin use. If you are not allergic, I recommend that older people take one regular aspirin tablet (325 mg) daily.

Prevent Loneliness & Isolation

Socialization

S is for
Socialization

Successful aging does not necessarily mean longevity, but rather how well we meet our spiritual needs despite the consequences of normal physiological aging and the chronic diseases that affect our bodies. By *spiritual,* I mean a sense of being well centered, of believing that our lives have meaning, and of understanding the difference between liberty and freedom. Physical decline may impair our liberty by reducing our ability to go places and do things, but it need not impair our freedom to relate to others and the world around us. Organized religion is an important form of spirituality, but you can be spiritual without being religious.

Socialization refers to how we relate to one another. To age successfully, you must have a social domain; you must be meaningfully connected to other people. In my medical practice of providing care to older adults, I have seen many lonely and frail people enter the medical system through the emergency room or hospitalization because of their *social decline.* People who live by themselves, who have no families or whose families live elsewhere are often isolated from the rest of society. They are cloistered in their homes or apartments and have minimal contact with other human beings. Isolated, they become depressed, develop malnutrition and become weak and confused. They do not get needed medications and health care and are reluctant to ask neighbors for help. They do not know how to get help from community social services such as the Area Agency on Aging, Meals on Wheels, or the Transportation Authority. They are often at low-income levels where they have to decide whether to pay for medications, gas/electric/phone services, or food. This is not a description of just a few people; it describes far too many.

People who age successfully socialize. The rural elderly do not age as well as elderly people who live in towns and cities where they have public transportation, stores and friends. People who live with a spouse or companion age better than older singles. Older people who attend religious services age better than those who do not. (Although many older people with infirmities have a social decline because they can no longer attend worship services, some counteract that by following radio or TV services.)

Each of us has social needs we must fulfill if we are to age successfully. The healthcare system cannot meet these. The insurance carriers, including Medicare, cannot meet them. The good news is that nearly every community in the country has organizations and activities that meet older people's social needs. Learn about your Area Agency on Aging; it has a list of all the Senior Citizen Centers in your community. At Senior

Citizen Centers, you will make new friends and acquaintances as you relax or work in groups. You can learn how to use a computer, how to improve your driving skills and how to do scores of other good things in the company of others. Many communities have special opportunities for older people to return to school and even to earn a college degree. Community colleges offer many programs attractive to older people as do Institutes for Learning in Retirement.

Loneliness is one of the worst diseases an older person can get. No medicines or therapies can cure it. Lonely people have to cure themselves by increasing the amount of time they spend with others. Some people fight loneliness by getting a pet; having another living creature depend on them gives them a new purpose in life.

If your social needs are not met, you can develop significant physical decline, including malnutrition, skin breakdown and hip fracture. To age successfully, you must be mindful of your social health as well as your physical health.

What You Can Do

Talk to your neighbors. Schedule times to telephone or write to important people in your life. Get to know and make friends with your healthcare providers. I am really touched when I see that for a few of my patients, seeing the doctor is their *only* social outlet. That alone makes me glad I went to medical school.

There are many ways to enrich your social life. Call about opportunities at your church, synagogue or mosque; at your Area Agency on Aging and senior citizen centers; or at your school district. If you are invited to an event, go. You may have a great time! If you are having trouble with finances and can't pay your bills, ask for help.

They Really Do Help

Immunization

I is for
Immunization

Our immune systems are our natural defenses against diseases caused by viruses and bacteria. As we grow older, our immune systems weaken and we need vaccinations (that is, immunizations) to protect us.

IN A NUTSHELL:

- People 65 and older and all healthcare workers should have flu shots annually.
- People over 65 should have pneumonia vaccinations.
- People over 65 should have tetanus/diphtheria vaccinations.

VACCINATIONS AND THE IMMUNE SYSTEM
HOW THEY WORK

When we are vaccinated—that is, when we "get a shot" or take an oral vaccine—our immune systems learn how to recognize an invader bringing a serious disease into our bodies. For example, when we are vaccinated for a specific disease (measles, mumps, chicken pox, etc.), we get an *antigen*—a small amount of the virus or bacteria that causes that disease.

The immune system reacts to *antigens* by creating *antibodies* that will fight future invasions of that disease.

Immunizations against measles, mumps, rubella, chicken pox, polio and hepatitis A and B are now standard for infants and children. Because our immune systems weaken as we grow older, it is *very* important that older people have immunizations that protect them from the diseases especially common among that age group.

THREE *MUST HAVE* IMMUNIZATIONS FOR OLDER PEOPLE

INFLUENZA. Influenza is a serious illness that can result in death. Influenza vaccines are fairly effective in protecting against it and cause very few adverse reactions.

- Everyone aged 65 and older should have an annual flu shot.
- Healthcare workers, especially those who work in nursing homes, should have an annual flu shot.
- People younger than 65 who have severe, chronic conditions or weak immune systems should have an annual flu shot.

PNEUMONIA. Streptococcal pneumonia is a serious illness that can result in death. Although a pneumonococcal vaccine may not prevent pneumonococcal pneumonia, it will greatly reduce the harmful effects of streptococcal pneumonia.

- Everyone 65 and older should be immunized against pneumonococcal pneumonia. Revaccination every five years is recommended for people up to age 75.
- One revaccination should suffice for people whose last pneumonia vaccine occurred when they were under 65 and more than five years earlier.

TETANUS AND DIPTHERIA. Although they are rare in the United States, it is strongly recommended that older people be protected from these serious diseases. Some authorities recommend an initial immunization followed by a booster every 10 years. Others recommend only a single booster at age 65.

- If you haven't had the initial series of three tetanus/diphtheria immunizations, get them now.
- If you have had the initial three doses earlier, get a booster shot at age 65 or older.

SHINGLES. Shingles, also called Herpes Zoster, is a painful skin rash often accompanied by blisters. Other symptoms can include fever, headache, chills and upset stomach.

The vaccine for shingles, which was approved in 2006, is recommended for adults 60 and over. However, people who have had a life-threatening allergic reaction to gelatin, the antibiotic neomycin, or any other component of shingles vaccine should not take the vaccine. Consult with your doctor about side effects before you take the vaccine.

What You Can Do

Check with your doctor to be sure that you have the necessary immunizations and/or booster for Influenza, Pneumonia, Tetanus and Diphtheria.

Are You A Safe Driver?

Car Crashes

C is for

Car Crash

Natural declines in our physical abilities make older drivers- say, 70 and above- more prone to have car accidents. Although most of us can't avoid these declines, we are aware of them and adjust our driving habits accordingly.

We drive fewer miles and shorter distances. We drive at slower speeds. We avoid driving at night or in bad weather. We wait for longer gaps before turning across and merging into traffic.

An increasing number of older adults are involved in motor vehicle accidents, many of which are fatal. Teenage drivers and older adults are the two groups with the highest incidence of motor vehicle accidents. In 1998, 13 million Americans aged 70 and over were driving . By 2020, more than 20 million Americans aged 70 and over will be driving.

- On the basis of per-vehicle miles driven, older drivers have more frequent car incidents. *Drivers in the 85 and older group are three times more likely to have car accidents than drivers in lower age groups*

- Of all the people involved in car accidents, older people are more likely to be killed. By age 85, the driver fatality rate is the highest of all age groups.

NATURAL DECLINES IN PHYSICAL CONDITION MAKE OLDER DRIVERS MORE VULNERABLE TO AUTO ACCIDENTS

Hearing. As we age, our hearing weakens. We are less likely to hear an ambulance or police siren and know where it is coming from. We are less likely to hear a car or truck approaching from the rear. In short, we are less likely to pick up sounds that could warn us of potential danger.

Vision. As we age, our vision weakens. We don't see as sharply as younger drivers. Glare bothers us. Night driving strains us. Our field of vision tends to narrow. We are less sharp in sensing the presence of other vehicles, their speeds, and their movements in relation to ours.

Mental Changes. As we age, we are more likely to have some memory loss and forget that a particular intersection is especially dangerous or that a corner that had no stop sign for years now has one. Our reaction time and judgment may be impaired. (*Example: You are about to make a left turn onto a two-way street. How far away is that car coming toward you? How fast is it going? Do you have enough time to make the turn or should you wait until that car passes? And what about the car* *coming the other way?* As we age, it takes us longer to answer these questions correctly).

Weakness in the legs, ankles, and knees. Strokes and arthritic changes in the spine and lower extremities can result in weaknesses that slow reaction times on the gas and brake pedals.

OTHER FACTORS THAT MAKE OLDER DRIVERS MORE VULNERABLE TO AUTO ACCIDENTS

Medications and Drugs. Medications and drugs increase the risk of auto accidents. Many Americans take Benzodiazepines, a class of tranquilizing drug that includes Valium, Ativan, Librium, Dalmane, Xanax and Restoril. The use of these drugs increases with age: 35% of all Benzodiazepine prescriptions written in the United States are for people aged 60 and over (17% of the total population). In a randomized controlled study of younger drivers, a single 10-milligram dose of Valium lowered their open-road driving performance to a level consistent with the effects of a legally intoxicating alcohol blood level. The assumption is that a 10-milligram dose of Valium would have even worse effects on older drivers.

Yet on any given day, *one of every five drivers on the road is taking a Benzodiazepine despite packaged insert warnings to avoid these medications while driving.*

Alcohol. The slogan *Don't Drink and Drive* is especially applicable to older people. The body absorbs and processes alcohol into muscle mass. Because muscle mass decreases as we age, alcohol has a greater negative effect on older people. Just one drink will affect an older person more than it will a younger one.

Alcohol greatly increases the risk of auto accidents across all ages of drivers. Yet on any given day, *one in ten drivers is under the influence of alcohol.*

What You Can Do

1. **See your eye doctor at least once a year.** Make sure you are tested for cataracts and glaucoma. Ask for visual field testing.

2. **Ask a younger person to evaluate your driving and sign up for the AARP 55 *Alive* Driving Program.**

3. **Review all your medications with your doctor, especially sleeping pills and nerve pills.** Refrain from driving if you must take these. Ask a friend to give you a ride.

4. **Don't drink alcohol and drive.**

5. **Exercise at least 3 - 5 times a week.** Walking is excellent. Ask about lower extremity strength training programs.

6. **If you suffer from memory impairment, never drive alone.** Always have someone else in the car who can help if the need arises. Many states require doctors to report patients with memory loss to the Department of Motor Vehicles. These people may be forbidden to drive. This is not a punitive measure, but rather a step to protect both the memory-impaired person and others on the road.

7. **Always wear your seat belt and see that your passengers wear theirs.**

8. **Keep children in the back seat.**

Heart Disease The #1 Killer

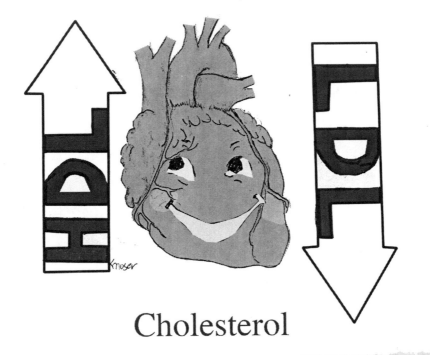

Cholesterol

C is for

Cholesterol and Other Lipids

This section describes in clear, easy-to-understand language what all the talk about cholesterol means. Don't be put off by unfamiliar words like lipids and triglycerides. Just read the material here and learn how to age successfully by dealing with any cholesterol-related problems you may have.

Lipids are the fats found in our blood. They include cholesterol and triglycerides. The two important kinds of cholesterol are:

High-Density Lipoproteins or *HDL's.* These are the "good" cholesterols.

Low-Density Lipoproteins or *LDL's.* These are the "bad" cholesterols.

If your cholesterol levels are abnormal, you run the risk of serious heart and artery diseases. You should maintain these cholesterol levels:

HDL: More than 40 mg for men; more than 50 mg for women

LDL: Less than 70 mg for those with established coronary artery disease and diabetes; less than 100 mg for all others

Triglyceride: Less than 150 mg

Fortunately, there are simple and effective ways to treat abnormal lipid levels. But first, you have to know what your lipid levels are. People over 20 should have lab work to measure their lipid levels at least every five years. Older people should ask their physicians about more frequent testing.

If your lipid levels are not within acceptable ranges, your doctor can help you by recommending life style changes (diet, weight management, exercise) and, perhaps, medication.

If you have high LDL, low HDL and high triglycerides, it is best to begin by lowering the LDL level, then lowering the triglyceride level and finally raising the HDL level.

MEDICATIONS

Medicines that manage lipid levels include statins, bile acid seqestrants, nicotinic acid, and fibric acids.

Statins. Zocor, Lipitor, Mevacor, Pravachol, Crestor and Lestol are available. Discuss with your physician which ones will help reduce LDL, increase HDL and decrease triglycerides. Side effects can include muscle pain and weakening and liver inflammation. You should not take statins if you have active or chronic liver disease. Here is an explanation of the medicines that manage lipid levels.

Bile Acid Sequestrants. Prevalie, Colestid and WelChol can reduce LDL significantly and increase HDL slightly. They may have no effect on triglycerides, or they may affect them adversely. Side effects can include upset stomach, constipation and decreasing the effectiveness of other drugs you might be taking. You should not take bile acids if your triglyceride level is over 400.

Nicotinic Acid. Niaspan, Niacor and Slo-Niacin can reduce LDL and triglyceride levels and increase HDL levels. Side effects can include flushing, hyperglycemia (too much sugar in the blood), gout, upset stomach and inflammation of the liver. You should not take nicotinic acid drugs if you have chronic liver disease, severe gout, diabetes, or peptic ulcer disease.

Fibric Acids. Lopid, Tricor and Atromide-S can reduce LDL (except in some patients with high triglycerides), increase HDL and lower triglycerides. Side effects can include muscle pain, indigestion and gall stones. You should not take fibric acids if you have severe kidney or blood disease.

Also, Stanol and Sterolesters (plant estrogens) are now incorporated into food products such as margarine (eg, Benecol) to help lower LDL and raise HDL.

What You Can Do

Have your lipid levels checked on the schedule your doctor sets and have your doctor determine the therapy that will benefit you most. This therapy should follow the National Cholesterol Education Program (NCEP) guidelines.

Remember that a sensible diet, weight management and exercise may be the best ways to control your lipid levels.

You Can Prevent Strokes

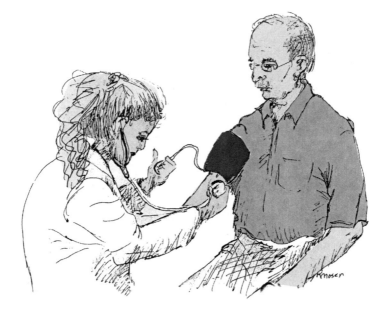

Blood Pressure

P is for

Pressure

Blood pressure, that is. Here are some simple facts that you must know about high blood pressure, which is often called **hypertension:**

- High blood pressure can cause a heart attack
- High blood pressure can cause a stroke
- High blood pressure can damage your kidneys
- You can do a lot to control your blood pressure

What is blood pressure? Our hearts are pumps that send blood through our arteries. Blood pressure measures how swiftly or slowly the blood is flowing. Depending on activity and stress, our blood pressure can vary throughout the day.

How we measure it. As blood flows through our arteries, it pushes against the inside of the artery walls. When these walls are relaxed or open, the pressure is lower than it is when they are narrowed or constricted. Blood pressure is higher as the heart beats to send blood out through the arteries. That pressure is called *systolic.* Blood pressure is lower when the heart rests as it fills with blood again. That pressure is called *diastolic.*

We measure in terms of systolic over diastolic. A healthy young adult has a blood pressure of about 110/75. By age 60, average blood pressure is about 140/70. However, the "ideal" blood pressure is less than 120/80, according to the Joint National Committee guidelines.

High blood pressure and older people. Hypertension is common among older adults. Twenty-five percent of retirement community and nursing home residents have high blood pressure. Follow these *Nine Guides to Handling High Blood Pressure* to reduce your chances of having high blood pressure lead to serious illness and/or premature death:

1. **Have Your Blood Pressure Taken Periodically.**
    Have a blood pressure reading at least once a year. This can be done at home, in your doctor's office, in a clinic, and in many other settings, including health fairs and malls.
    If you are diagnosed as having high blood pressure (hypertension) but your pressure is below 140/90, you should have at least one more reading greater than 120/80 to confirm the diagnosis. This is important because older people who are treated for hypertension after a misdiagnosis can have severe adverse effects.
    If, however, your first reading suggests severe hypertension—that is, a reading greater

than 160/100—you should begin treatment immediately.

2. **Within four weeks of having been diagnosed as having hypertension have these necessary additional diagnostic tests:**

- Urinalysis
- Complete blood count
- Serum sodium, potassium and creatinine
- Uric acid infesting glucose
- Electrocardiogram
- Fasting glucose
- Lipid profile

These tests identify both the secondary and primary causes of an individual's hypertension.

3. **If you are diagnosed as having hypertension, be sure your doctor checks for other heart attack risk factors. These include:**

- High cholesterol readings
- Diabetes
- Cigarette smoking
- Overweight or obesity
- Family history of heart attacks

4. **If you are diagnosed as having mild hypertension, (blood pressure between 120/80-140/90), cut back on salt.**

Lower alcohol consumption if you take more than two drinks a day.

Lose weight, especially if you are more than 10% over your ideal body weight.

If you have other risk factors like diabetes, a history of heart attack, stroke, or kidney disease, you may need medications even at this level of blood pressure.

5. **If after cutting back on salt and losing weight you remain hypertensive, begin medications that reduce blood pressure.** Such medications significantly reduce heart attacks and strokes.

6. **If your physician prescribes blood pressure reduction medication, understand what type you will use.** Try to avoid short-acting ones; longer-acting medications taken once or twice a day are more effective.

7. **If diuretics (water pills) or an ACE inhibitor are prescribed for you, have your serum sodium, potassium and creatinine levels checked within one week of starting those medications.** This can decrease your serum sodium level, lower your potassium level and change the way your kidneys function.

8. **Ask your doctor if you show any signs of kidney damage.** If you do, see whether an angiotensin

converting enzyme (ACE) inhibitor is a desirable blood pressure reduction medicine for you. These medications preserve kidney functioning.

9. **Be sure to tell your doctor if you have any breathing problems.** Some blood pressure reduction medicines called beta-blockers can cause harmful side effects in asthmatic patients.

What You Can Do

Review the <u>Nine</u> <u>Steps</u> just listed and remember that high blood pressure (hypertension) is extremely common in older persons. It may be the most common condition nationally. It is easily treated, but if it is **NOT** treated, it can cause serious illness and premature death.

Multiple Diseases - Multiple Doctors
Multiple Medications

Rx/Medications

R is for Rx:

Prescriptions and Medicines

For many older people, this may be the most important section in *BASIC PREVENTION*. Here's why:

Americans take a lot of prescribed and over-the-counter drugs without thinking very much about their effects on our bodies. As we grow older, we take more. We often develop chronic conditions-visual problems, arthritis, hypertension, diabetes, etc.- that require medication. Many of us, as we age, may develop diseases (heart disease, kidney impairment, osteoporosis and others) that also require medication. Although older adults make up only 14% of the U.S. population, people over 65 consume more than 30% of all prescribed drugs.

BUT… certain aspects of the aging process that occur in the young-old are magnified in the old-old and make older people vulnerable to harmful drug side effects. As we age:

- Our kidneys become less efficient in eliminating drugs through urination.
- Changes in the way our livers function reduce their ability to process drugs.

- Our bodies can increase the effects of fat-soluble drugs and also increase the effects of water-soluble ones.
- Changes in the sensitivity of body sites where drugs go can change the drugs' effectiveness.

Common side effects of drugs include:

- **Confusion**
- **Forgetfulness**
- **Unsteady walking and falls**
- **Fatigue**
- **Urinary or GI (gastrointestinal) disturbance**
- **Constipation**
- **Parkinsonian side effects (tremors, shuffling gait and poor posture)**

All too frequently, patients and caregivers, including physicians, mistake these side effects as the symptoms of a new illness or the normal effects of the aging process. Such mistakes are tragic. Here's how to avoid them:

1. When your doctor prescribes a medication, *ASK:*
- How should I react to the drug? (Especially important if you are taking other medications.)
- Is it safe to take with the other drugs I'm taking?
- How long should I take it?
- How long should I take the other drugs I'm now taking?

- Does this medication require monitoring?
  Medications such as blood thinners (Warfarin
  or Coumadin) require periodic blood testing.
  Diuretics (water pills) require tests that measure
  the chemical (sodium and potassium) levels
  in your blood. Unmonitored, diuretics can
  cause irregular heart rhythm and confusion.
  For heart disease and hypertension, doctors
  often prescribe a drug known as an angiotensin
  converting enzyme inhibitor. This requires a
  periodic kidney function test.

2. Insist that your doctor or pharmacist explain to
   you the purpose of the drug.
   Know what your reaction to a medication should
   be and discuss this with your doctor. Are you
   having the expected reactions? Are you having
   side effects?

3. Write out your medication list on a card that
   you can fold and keep in your wallet or purse.
   Keep your list up to date and review it regularly
   with your doctor. This will help stopping
   medications you no longer need. (Up to 2/3 of
   all medications taken by people 80 or older are
   actually unnecessary.) Make copies and keep one in
   a tube or jar in your freezer along with your Living

Will/Advance Directive. This is where emergency personnel will look if you are unconscious.

4. Ask your doctor if any of your medications have strong anti-cholinergic qualities. Such drugs include diphenhydramine (a drug common to most cold preparations), Benadryl other anti-histamines and certain anti-depressants. Anti-cholinergic medications can cause confusion, urine retention, constipation, dry mouth and dry eyes and can be potentially very dangerous to older people.

    They should be used with great care, and you and your doctor should be aware of harmful side effects, including loss of balance. Many of these compounds are present in over-the-counter drugs. Whatever medications you buy, prescription or over the counter, always ask your pharmacist about potential side effects.

5. Avoid taking barbiturate medications. Ask your doctor and/or pharmacist if the prescribed drug is a barbiturate.

6. If you need medication for severe pain, ask if the medication is Demerol. This drug causes spells of significant confusion. Avoid it and ask your doctor for something more suitable.

7. Be a partner with your doctor and your pharmacist and schedule a regular review of your medications.

What You Can Do

Take the cotton out of the bottle when you get your medicine home. By absorbing moisture, the cotton accelerates the medicine's breakdown.

Don't take medicines that have an unfamiliar or peculiar odor. Take them back to the drug store and get the pharmacist's opinion.

Don't take outdated medicines. On average, a medicine loses about 10% of its effectiveness in a year. An outdated medicine might not hurt you, but it won't be as effective as it should be.

Before accepting a prescription from your doctor, ask if it is absolutely necessary. Sometimes there are ways to treat a condition without drugs. Ice packs and warm compresses are effective at treating sprains and strains. With them, you may not need aspirins or other compounds that can result in stomach ulcers and bruising.

Don't double up on the next pill if you miss a dose of your medicine. If you miss one, just continue the normal sequence your doctor prescribed.

Never give your medicines to a neighbor. Although some older adults share medicines to save money, it's a bad practice. Remember that the pharmacist keeps a record of what you should take. If you share, those records are inaccurate and won't help you or your doctor if you need to review your medication history.

Review all of your medications with your doctor frequently and cut out the ones that aren't absolutely necessary. (One activity of a geriatrician is to review patients' medications.)

Get to know your pharmacist. Go to the same pharmacist consistently so that he or she can keep a complete record, often on a computer, of your medication history.

Don't drink alcohol when you are taking any medications. Alcohol itself is a drug that doesn't mix well with other drugs. It can make you confused and disoriented.

Remember that cigarette smoking increases the effects of many medications.

A normal dose for a non-smoker may not be sufficient for a smoker.

Never leave your doctor's office if you can't read his/ her writing on your prescription. If you can't read it, your pharmacist may not be able to either. Ask your doctor to print the information so that it's legible to you and your pharmacist. If this request annoys your doctor, it may be time to consider another one.

Don't call your doctor for a refill at the last minute. It's unfair to call after office hours and on weekends for refills when you know well in advance when your medications will run out. Be responsible and call for your refills in a timely fashion. (And if you are regularly responsible, unanticipated urgent issues will be treated more respectfully.)

Six Hours a Week

Exercise

E is for

Exercise

Have no doubt about it: Exercise will help you lead a longer, healthier (and probably happier) life. The other side of the coin is that inactivity—being a couch potato—is the kiss of death for older people. This part of BASIC PREVENTION will tell you what kind of and how much exercise you need.

But first look at what exercise can do for older people. Physically fit older adults are less likely to suffer from:

- Heart disease
- Hypertension
- Obesity
- Mental health disorders
- Osteoporosis
- Diabetes

Lack of exercise leads to:

- Loss of muscle mass
- Worsening of arthritis
- Constipation
- Diabetes
- Hip and other bone fractures
- Loss of bone strength

- Depression
- Obesity
- Imbalance and falls

Although every older person should have an exercise program, be sure to discuss your exercise plans with your doctor. If you have two risk factors for heart disease, your doctor may recommend a cardiac stress test before you begin an exercise program. The risk factors are

- Previous history of heart disease
- Diabetes
- Hypertension
- Obesity
- High serum cholesterol
- Strong family history of heart disease

How much exercise do you need? You don't have to jog for miles and lift weights for hours. I recommend that you exercise for six hours—that's 360 minutes—a week. Since three 20-minute exercise sessions will do as much for you as one 60-minute one, I recommend that you schedule three twenty-minute sessions a day. If you do that for six days, you've met the 360 minutes recommendation.

Before you start, check with an exercise trainer or a physical therapist. Your doctor can recommend the right person or program for you.

What kind of exercise do you need? There are four kinds, and you should have some of each.

They are: resistance training, endurance training, balance training and flexibility training.

Let's take them one at a time.

RESISTANCE TRAINING. This will increase the strength and even the mass of your muscles. Exercising the large muscles in your arms, shoulders and legs will help you rise out of a chair, climb stairs and perform the routine activities of daily living in later life.

Resistance training programs may use Dynabands (large rubber bands that provide you with varying degrees of resistance), free weights, Nautilus equipment or even isometric exercises. Since isometric exercises can be especially stressful to the cardiovascular system, I do not recommend them for older people).

For older people, I recommend starting off with 1- 2- or 3- pound hand weights. With these, you can do one set (a set is 8 – 10 lifts of the weights) of upper-body work. Then tie the weights to your feet to do lower bodywork. Over time, increase to 5- to 10- pound weights. Increase gradually to two sets and finally to three sets of 8-10 repetitions. By increasing the weight, you cause the muscles to become exhausted more quickly, and that builds muscle mass.

Weight lifting combines Resistance Training with Endurance Training. Frequent repetitions of low weight lifting will increase your endurance. Increasing the amount of weight you lift increases your resistance and builds more muscle mass.

ENDURANCE TRAINING. In addition to improving the way your muscles and joints function, Endurance Training strengthens your heart and your lungs. You can get these benefits by walking, riding a bike or dancing. The important thing is to get up and get going!

If you are out of shape, you can start to build endurance by walking half a mile. If this sounds like too much, try a quarter mile or just a daily walk around the block to get started. As you build endurance, walk a little longer until you can walk one mile in 18 minutes. After eight weeks, your goal should be to walk two miles in 35-40 minutes. The ideal goal is to walk three miles in 45 minutes, but that really is an ideal. Most older people are not able to do it.

Riding a stationery exercise bicycle can improve both the endurance of your frontal thigh muscles and your sense of balance. Walking on a treadmill will increase the endurance of other muscle groups and strengthen your heart.

You should build both lower and upper body endurance. Upper-body endurance exercises include rowing, hand pedaling a bicycle, dancing and even orchestra conducting. You do this in front of your stereo!

Each of these endurance activities will improve your coordination, which the normal aging process diminishes.

Riding a bike is a challenge for some older people. Riding a bike can improve both your endurance and your balance.

Try to do some of your Endurance Training with a group; that way you can increase your social encounters. And be sure to take time to stretch your muscles (Flexibility Training) before you walk or ride.

BALANCE TRAINING. When you lose your sense of balance, your brain is no longer sure of where your body is in space. This weakness can result from diabetes or chronic arthritis, especially of the spine and neck. You can start to sense where your body is in space by sitting in a chair, lifting your legs and concentrating on what muscle is doing the lifting for you.

People who need balance training may start exercising with a short program of simply walking around a block where the surface is smooth and flat. This will help sharpen the sense of balance as it also improves endurance. The walker should focus on where her/his body is in space.

Tai-Chi is excellent training for improving balance, but these programs are not always available to older people.

FLEXIBILITY TRAINING. This involves s...t... r...e...t...c...h... i...n...g muscles and tendons and reaching every muscle that should be stretched.

For total body stretching, start with the head and work down to your shoulders and your arms. Stretch the large muscles. Then the small muscles. Now work down and stretch your leg muscles.

A proper stretching program will loosen up your muscles, improve your arthritis, and break-up little crusts that over time can develop on muscles.

What You Can Do

An exercise trainer or a physical therapist can be highly valuable at teaching you how to perform exercises in the four categories. Your doctor can recommend a health club or program where you can get such help. Your doctor may not be able to write a prescription for physical therapy. In general, health plans reimburse only for physical therapy after an acute event or hospitalization.

Exercise with a group. You'll make new friends and the other participants will encourage you to meet your goals.

Exercise is *fun!* It's not a punishment. It's a powerful way to ward off immobility, falls, fractures and mental depression. If you have not been exercising, that means you have not been exercising **yet. Now is the time to start.**

Don't Fool Yourself

Vices

V is for

Vices: Tobacco, Alcohol, Drugs and Gambling

Misuse and outright abuse of tobacco, alcohol and illicit drugs are general public health concerns and have significant affects on the aging population. Although abuse problems are thought to effect people who use substances in high quantities and at regular intervals, older people can have harmful effects from moderate or even light use.

TOBACCO. There is no doubt about it: Tobacco use—especially cigarette, cigar and pipe smoking—increases your chances of having severe illness and dying from heart disease and lung cancer. Nicotine and other compounds found in tobacco are highly addictive substances, so addictive, in fact, that most smokers find it extremely difficult to stop.

People who smoke or live in a household where others smoke are at risk of developing frequent respiratory infections, heart disease and lung cancer. People, including those 70 and older, who stop smoking reduce those risks significantly.

Although we know how difficult it is for many people to stop smoking, it can be done.

When a person tells me "I can't stop smoking." I reply, "You haven't stopped smoking yet."

That **YET** is a powerful word. Remember that "cutting down" is not enough. There is evidence that even one cigarette a day can increase the risk of cancer tenfold. "Cutting out" is the goal.

If you smoke, now is the time to stop. Your doctor can help by recommending counseling sessions, withdrawal programs, and medications that ease the body's craving for nicotine.

Remember: If you are a smoker, you just haven't stopped YET. You can. And if you get some help, you will.

ALCOHOL. More than seven drinks a week is identified as "at risk drinking." This level can increase the risk for strokes, impair driving skills and can cause falls, breast cancer, and harmful interactions with some over-the-counter medications. (People who take blood thinners like Coumadin should not drink alcohol.)

Because our muscle mass decreases as we age, even lower amounts of alcohol can give us harmful effects. Alcohol is associated with liver failure, chronic obstructive pulmonary disease and peptic ulcer disease.

Alcohol-related problems are increasing in retirement communities, and more than (20% and as many as 50%) of admissions to acute care hospitals are the result of alcohol and other substances abuse. More than 10% of cars on the road are being driven by people under the influence of alcohol or another harmful substance.

About one in 10 individuals seen in doctors' offices is addicted to alcohol or drugs. They may suffer from gastritis (upset stomach), falls, dizziness, weight loss, depression, lung cancer and GI tract cancer. We need to screen patients in all settings for alcohol and drug-related disorders.

Some authorities say that an ounce of alcohol daily can protect the heart. Remember, however, that the benefit can be offset by side effects that include falls, gastritis and harmful interaction with other medications. My advice: If you don't drink, don't start now.

DRUGS. Cocaine, heroin and their derivatives are extremely harmful. Their use can destroy your life and your family's. Don't go near them.

Studies demonstrate that Marijuana impairs both lung and brain function. Don't kid yourself into thinking it's a harmless, recreational drug. Don't use it.

The chronic use of "nerve medications" such as Diazapan can increase the risk of falls, impair driving skills and cause depression and acutely confused states.

GAMBLING. There are increasing opportunities to gamble at casinos, lotteries, betting parlors, race tracks and the Internet. An increasing number of people, including older adults, are taking advantage of these opportunities. Is that bad? Not necessarily. Games of chance can be fun. But when gambling goes too far, it can hurt not only your pocketbook but also your health.

Here is the National Council on Problem Gambling's answer to the question, What is problem gambling?

Problem gambling is gambling behavior which causes disruptions in any major area of life: psychological, physical, social, or vocational. The term problem gambling includes, but is not limited to, the condition known as "Pathological or Compulsive Gambling," a progressive addiction characterized by increasing preoccupation with gambling, a need to bet more money more frequently, restlessness or irritability when attempting to stop, "chasing" losses, and loss of control manifested by continuation of the gambling behavior in spite of mounting, serious negative consequences.

What You Can Do

Don't use tobacco. If you smoke now, commit yourself to stopping. You can do it!

If you drink alcohol, do so moderately and don't exceed seven drinks spread over a week.

Don't even think of using cocaine, heroin, or their derivatives. Don't use marijuana.

Regularly review the medications, prescription and over-the-counter drugs with your doctor and cut out the ones that aren't necessary.

If you think you may be a problem gambler, GET HELP! Call the National Council on Problem Gambling at 1-202-547-9204. Their web site is www.ncpgambling.org.

Earth Belongs To Our Children

Environment

E is for

Environment

Most of us think of the environment in terms of air, water and natural resources. That is the *Universal Environment*, and I will refer to it at the end of this section.

Older adults should also be concerned about their *Personal Environment*. Paying attention to it can help you avoid unnecessary injuries. Your *Personal Environment* is where you live. Let's walk through it room by room and see what you can do to make it as safe as possible.

YOUR PERSONAL ENVIRONMENT
BATHROOM

- The tub or shower should have handrails and non-skid pads.
- Replace slippery bathroom mats with non-slip ones.
- A raised toilet seat can prevent falls.
- Lighting should be on the bright side.
- If you are buying a new home, be sure that a wheel chair or walker fit in the bathroom.

- Remove hazardous materials under the sink that could be mistaken for mouthwash. (detergents, Liquid Plumber, etc.)
- Empty the medicine cabinet of outdated prescriptions, unprotected razor blades and other sharp objects

BEDROOM

- Remove throw rugs that people can slip on.
- Don't have electrical wires/cords or telephone wire run across doorways.
- Have a smoke detector nearby. (Remember to keep the batteries fresh. Replace them twice a year when the time changes to or from Daylight Savings.
- Know how you will escape if there is a fire.
- If a disabled person uses the room, have a marker noting that on the window. This will help firemen if there is a fire.
- There should be enough room for a person with a wheelchair or walker to turn around.
- Lighting should be sufficient.

STAIRWELL

- There should be at least one handrail. You may consider having two - one on each side.

- Lighting should be sufficient.
- The stair treads should be tightly fastened to the steps.
- People with poor depth perception need markers that show where the steps begin.
- Have a smoke detector with fresh batteries.

LIVING ROOM and DINING ROOM

- Remove throw rugs that people can slip on.
- Remove low-lying furniture such as coffee tables with sharp edges. People with poor vision can hurt themselves by bumping into them.
- Have a carbon monoxide detector nearby.
- If you have a wood-burning stove or fireplace, a smooth transition from the carpet to the tile or hardwood floor will prevent falls.

KITCHEN

- Have a smoke detector with fresh batteries.
- Remove hazardous chemicals from underneath the kitchen sink.
- Clean the refrigerator of moldy foods and stale milk.
- Make sure the refrigerator light is working.
- Make sure the stove is in safe working condition.

- Have friends or neighbors help you reach items stored on hard-to-reach high shelves.
- Have a working fire extinguisher suitable for kitchen fires.
- Remove slippery mats and throw rugs.
- Keep food and water bowls for pets in corners where you won't trip over them.
- Don't let pets be constantly underfoot.
- Arrange cutlery so you won't cut yourself when you reach into a drawer.
- Have a plan of escape should there be a first-floor fire.

BASEMENT

- Prevent scalds by reducing your hot-water tank temperature to 120 degrees Fahrenheit.
- Have smoke detectors with fresh batteries and fire alarms in place.
- Make sure the basement steps are adequately lighted.
- Make sure the basement steps handrails are adequate.
- Make sure the treads on the steps are firmly anchored.
- Keep a telephone in the basement in case you fall and need help.

- Make sure your heating system is in good working condition.
- Have a carbon monoxide detector in the basement.
- Have your home inspected for radon emissions.
- Remove old newspapers and other hazardous materials such as paint cans, old detergents and other flammable products.
- Have an escape plan if you are in the basement when a house fire breaks out.

GARAGE

- Doors should be in good working order.
- Remove old gas cans, fertilizer, lime and other combustible or caustic products.
- Have a smoke detector and fire alarm.
- Remove oil or other slippery substances from the floor.
- Make sure there is room for you to get in and out of your car safely.

These are potentially hazardous situations you can correct. Remember: An ounce of prevention is worth a pound of cure.

THE UNIVERSAL ENVIRONMENT

Humans have done great harm to our universal home, Planet Earth. We have polluted its oceans, rivers, lakes and streams. We have destroyed rain forests and upset the natural balance of almost every species in the animal kingdom. Toxic waste contaminates land and water, and our air is polluted. We have abused our natural resources. The ozone layer is thinning and global warming is apparent.

Our individual health requires a healthy universal environment. Now is the time to act.

What You Can Do

- Encourage your legislators to support environmentally conscious bills.
- Reduce your household waste. Reuse it. Recycle it.
- Buy environmentally sound products, including Ozone-safe ones.
- Buy products with environmentally friendly packaging.
- Be water conscious. Every drop counts. Restrict the time your water runs as you bathe, shave, brush your teeth, do dishes, wash clothes and water the lawn.

Planet Earth is the only home we have. Keeping it healthy will keep us healthy.

You Are What You Eat

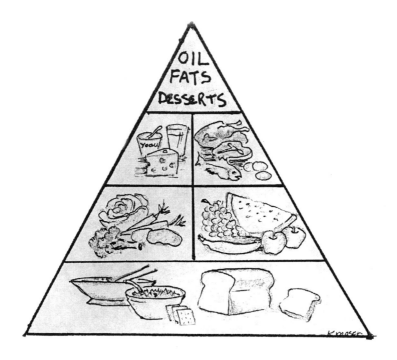

Nutrition

N is for

Nutrition: How and What We Eat

Good eating habits will help you greatly on the road to successful aging.

Nutritional needs vary. Babies' needs are different from teenagers'; men's are different from women's; small people's are different from large ones'. But certain things are constant. Poor nutrition can lead to illnesses and their complications. Good nutrition can make us healthier and stronger.

As we grow older, our lean body mass (muscle mass) decreases and our body fat increases. As a result, we need fewer calories. In addition, our need for carbohydrates, fats and proteins changes as we grow older. Chronic diseases can affect the kinds of food we can or cannot eat. And finally, medications we take can interfere with the body's ability to absorb nutrients. In short, many factors influence our nutritional health.

There is a widespread lack of understanding about nutrition. Advertising—fast food chains, pizza, alcohol-has markedly (and negatively) influenced our eating habits. Americans may eat a lot but, in general, we eat badly. Add to that the fact that we don't exercise. We drive rather than walk; we sit before TV screens, movie screens and computer monitors. That's why a majority of Americans are significantly overweight and many are grossly obese. This increases their risk of hypertension, diabetes, heart attacks, strokes, emphysema, and cancer.

A word about dieting. The craze for dieting in the United States has reached epidemic proportions. Think of the TV, radio and newspaper ads for "quick and easy" weight loss. Although we have almost no scientific knowledge about these programs, they are advertised as gospel truth. *Don't be taken in by these false claims.*

Will poor nutrition increase *your* risk of developing serious health problems? Take this little quiz for an answer.

NINE NUTRITION QUESTIONS
(Answer YES or NO to each of the following)

1. Do you have an illness that has changed the amount of food you eat?

2. Do you eat only one meal a day?

3. Does your diet have few fruits, vegetables, or milk products?

4. Do you have three or more drinks of alcohol per day?

5. Do you have dental problems that make it hard to eat?

6. Do you sometimes not have enough money to buy the food you need?

7. Do you eat alone most of the time?

8. Do you take three or more medications per day?

9. Have you unintentionally lost or gained six pounds in one month, ten pounds in two or three months?

Scoring
YES ANSWERS

3	Some Risk
3- 5	Moderate Risk
6 or More	High Risk. See a physician or dietitian.

CHOOSING YOUR DIET

Your diet should be well balanced. It should include fruits, vegetables and whole grains and be relatively low in fat. Choose lean meats and make sure that each portion is no larger than a deck of playing cards—that's about four ounces of meat and it's more than enough protein. Vary your meats and at times use fish and poultry instead. Eating salmon once or twice a week will help your heart.

Foods that are rich in antioxidant vitamins help prevent or repair the damage that oxygen can do to your body's cells. You have seen the effects of oxidation. Rust on a car or a sliced apple turning brown are examples. Internal oxidation in your body can damage cells and bring on many of the common problems associated with aging. (It is paradoxical that oxygen, the element that keeps us alive, also poses a major threat to our bodies.) High levels of antioxidants prevent the clogging of arteries and thus prevent heart attacks and strokes. They reduce cataracts (about two-thirds of Americans over 60 have cataracts). They reduce the complications of diabetes. Many fruits, vegetables and whole grains are rich in antioxidant vitamins. More than 80% of Americans *do not eat enough of these foods!* You should have 5 – 9 servings of fruits and vegetables and 6 – 11 servings of whole grain daily.

An easy way to make sure your diet includes antioxidants is to be sure your plate has various colors on it. All the fruits in this list are high in antioxidants, with raisins having the highest: raisins, blueberries, blackberries, strawberries, raspberries, plums, oranges, red grapes and cherries.

Here are vegetables (listed in order of highest to lowest in antioxidants):

1. Kale
2. Spinach
3. Brussels Sprouts
4. Alfalfa Sprouts
5. Broccoli
6. Red Bell Peppers
7. Beets
8. Onions
9. Corn
10. Eggplant

Looking at both lists, you can see why I recommend eating a plateful of food that is rich in colors.

What You Can Do

Include the fruits and vegetables listed above in your diet. If you do, you won't be making a radical change. Instead, you will be returning to the naturally available foods we ate before the advent of processed foods, fast foods and the frenetic food advertising media campaigns.

Bite On This For A While

Teeth

T is for

Teeth and Mouth

Like the other parts of our bodies, our teeth are aging. Still, we can help them age successfully.

Missing teeth, tooth decay, dry mouth and periodontal disease (disease of the gums and bones where your teeth grow) **do not** represent normal aging. Older people should not take them for granted. If you have any of these symptoms, get help. See a dentist!

What you should know about the most common teeth problems:

Caries or *tooth decay.* Throughout our lives, bacteria attack our teeth and cause cavities and loss of calcium. Decay that occurs between fillings and a person's teeth is called *Recurrent Caries.* Since older people have more fillings than younger ones, they are more likely to have recurrent caries.

Older people also have more root decay, which can result in the loss of one or more teeth. This kind of infection can spread to other areas of the body, including the heart, lungs and replaced joints such as in the hip. People of almost any age can have caries, but this disease's harmful effects are far greater among older people.

Although caries can occur naturally, these risk factors encourage the disease: poor dental hygiene, frequent eating of sticky foods with high sugar content (cake, cookies, candy, etc.), infrequent visits to a dentist and a decrease in saliva.

Preventing or minimizing dental caries requires daily flossing and brushing with fluoride toothpaste, cutting back on sweet, sticky foods and seeking dental treatment as needed (removing very bad teeth, treating others with fillings or crowns and root canal work if needed).

(See the section on *SalivaryFunction and Aging* for dealing with a decreased salivary flow.)

Periodontal Disease. The bones and gums that hold your teeth are called the *Periodontum*. Periodontal disease begins when bacteria form plaque—that is, patches—on the teeth near the gums and the root surfaces. Gingivitis (*gingiva* is the medical word for gums) is a common form of periodontal disease where plaque is limited to the gums. Gingivitis occurs more frequently in older adults than in younger ones. Its symptoms are swelling in the gums and light bleeding during brushing. The treatment is to remove the plaque.

Periodontitis, where the inflammation extends to the bone, is a more serious form of periodontal disease. It can lead to the loosening of teeth and to their eventual loss. The prevention of gingivitis and periodontitis is largely a matter of good oral hygiene—daily flossing and brushing with fluoride—and regular dental examinations and treatments as needed.

Toothlessness and dentures. In the 1960s, more than 70% of Americans over age 75 wore dentures (false teeth). By 1990, that figure was less than 40%. This was due to increased preventive and restorative dental care in childhood and early adulthood. Even so, many older people are unwilling or reluctant to pay for restorative dental treatment (treatment to save diseased teeth). When periodontal disease is unattended, teeth become loose, chewing becomes painful, and teeth can be lost.

Some people don't worry about their teeth, thinking that they can always get dentures. You should know that although dentures are helpful, they also have drawbacks. Denture wearers must chew more times before they can swallow. The range of foods they can eat is narrowed (no more corn on the cob for some) and, as a result, they may get less carbohydrates and proteins. Dentures can be a source of discomfort and embarrassment for older people and may require frequent adjustments by professionals.

Dentures require daily care. They are expensive and not covered by many health plans. They may have to be replaced if you lose weight. In short, do **all** you can to retain your **natural** teeth. Visit your dentist regularly.

Salivary function and aging. By keeping our mouths lubricated with fluid, salivation protects the tissue in our mouths. Saliva is necessary for chewing, swallowing and taste. It protects us from harmful bacteria. Our salivary glands provide adequate lubrication throughout our life spans. Certain conditions, however, including dehydration or medication side effects, can cause dry mouth (the medical term is *Xerostomia*) in older people. Dry mouth is often caused by prescription or over-the-counter medications that are anticholinergic, such as antihistamines, tricyclic antidepressants and opiates. More than 72% of nursing home patients receive between one and five such medicines. About 55% of older outpatients take these medicines.

There are many other causes of dry mouth: blockages in the salivary glands, depression, diabetes mellitus and radiation therapy for tumors of the mouth and tongue. Dry mouth causes rapidly destructive tooth decay, painful oral mucousitis and poor nutritional status.

Dry mouth should be prevented. If it occurs, its cause should be diagnosed properly. Medications that do not cause dry mouth can be substituted for those that do. Patients who suffer dry mouth from radiation therapy can now be treated successfully. See your doctor to ask about options.

Oral Cancers. Oral cancers are painless. They appear as red, white or red and white areas of the oral mucous membranes which may be ulcerated. If you see an area like this in your mouth, see your doctor or dentist immediately. Early diagnosis and treatment improves the outcome significantly.

Bad Breath. Bad breath or *halitosis* is common in younger and older adults. It occurs more frequently among older people because, due to their loss of taste receptors, they like sweet foods. Bad breath is caused by sugar fermenting on the tongue and gums. You can minimize or avoid it by cleaning your tongue thoroughly three or four times a day. Also, avoid milk products, candies, cakes, cookies, soft drinks, and other items with high sugar content.

Loss of Taste. Finally, there are changes in the sensations of smell and taste. Older adults with a diminished sense of smell frequently do not recognize when food is spoiled. People with a diminished sense of taste tend to over salt their food. Causes of loss of flavor include normal physiological changes, changes in memory and thinking, and the effects of medications. If you experience any decline in any one of these areas, please consult with your physician. Help is available for all of these problems.

What You Can Do

Do not take your teeth and mouth for granted. They are important for both your physical and social well-being. They are important on your journey to age successfully.

30% of People Age 70 Fall Each Year

Immobility & Falls

I is for
Immobility and Falls

When you were a small child, you probably fell a lot. Most young children do, and their falls tend not to cause great harm. Young adults and people in middle life fall, too, but not with troublesome frequency.

Among adults 65 and over, however, it's a different story. We fall more. One out of three older people will fall in the course of a year, and our falls have serious effects. People under 65 have 1.5 deaths per year per 100,000 persons due to falls. Although the 65 and over group represents 12% of the U.S. population, falls among that group represent *70% of all deaths due to falls.* People over 85 have *147 deaths per year per 100,000 persons due to falls.*

Although most of us fear that falling will cause a fracture (a broken bone), only 5 -10% of falls among older people result in serious injuries. Between 30 and 40% of older people who fall sustain bumps and abrasions, cuts, sprains, or strains. These soft tissue injuries can be debilitating and lead to decreased activity and increased days in bed.

A fall that results in a bump on the head can affect brain function or be fatal. Older people's blood vessels crush or tear more easily than younger people's do. These bumps can cause blood to ooze into confined spaces in the skull. The increased pressure on the brain reduces the brain's sharpness and can cause death due to compression of the brain.

An older person who lives alone may fall, be unable to get up or call for help and lie unnoticed for several hours or even several days. When this happens, the person may suffer from hypothermia (long exposure to cold temperatures). Lying in one position for a long time can destroy muscle tissue, which can lead to a massive concentration of protein in the kidneys that causes kidney failure.

Older people can become unnaturally afraid of falling and lose their confidence in being able to live normally. Some are afraid to leave their room or their home. Some become clinically depressed. Some restrict their social activities. These situations affect families, who worry and don't know how to respond to such fears.

Sometimes an older person who falls is put into a nursing home. That is frequently not a good solution to the problem.

WHICH IS MORE IMPORTANT: DID YOU HURT YOURSELF? or WHY DID YOU FALL?

They are both important, but we should always pay attention to the possible causes of a fall. Falls in older people should be recognized as a sign of functional decline and may represent the first sign of a serious illness. Falls are often the first tip-off to impending heart failure, pneumonia, urinary tract infection and other illnesses common to older people.

Many of the normal changes that occur in our bodies over time can lead to a fall. These changes include a decrease in muscle mass and strength, decrease in body water that can cause a sudden drop in blood pressure, diminished sensitivity that can bring on dizziness when changing position, and loss of bone mass. Other changes that make older people more vulnerable to falls are arthritis, reduced vision and reduced hearing. All these are part of normal aging.

Strokes and neurological conditions such as Parkinson's Disease can cause falls. The negative side effects of some medications can cause dizziness and light-headedness that bring on falls. (See Rx for Medications.)

But the most common cause of falls is accidents. Many of these occur in the home and are caused by the home environment: poor lighting, slippery throw rugs, low lying furniture and the lack of grab bars in bathtubs and showers.

Here is a breakdown of the causes of falls among older people:

1. ACCIDENTS /ENVIRONMENT........ 37%
2. PATHOLOGIES:
weakness, balance, and gait problems 12%

sudden unexplained falls.....................……..11%

dizziness and vertigo ....…....…........8%

sudden drop in blood pressure 5%

diseases of the brain ....…...........…..1%

other causes including acute illness,

confusion, poor eyesight, and drugs ...…....18%

Here is a checklist of common hazards linked to falls in the home.

Take the time to review the hazards/modifications clusters and make the recommended modifications in your home to significantly reduce the probability of falls.

HAZARDS	RECOMMENDED MODIFICATIONS
Lighting Problems	
Poor access to switches/ lamps	Provide ample lighting in rooms and hallways. Locate switches at room entrances
Low lighting	Provide extra lighting between bedroom and bathroom, at one or two step elevation changes, and at the top and bottom of stairwells. Use 100 to 200 watt bulbs and 3-way bulbs
Lack of night lights	Use nightlights in darkened rooms

Glare	Use translucent light shades and frosted bulbs. Avoid exposed light bulbs
Floor and Hallway Problems	
Clutter	Arrange furniture so that pathways are clear
Low Lying Objects	Remove low-lying objects (e.g., coffee tables and magazine racks.)
Limited walking space	Provide stable furniture that people can hold onto along pathways
Waxed/wet floors	Use nonskid rugs and carpet runners on slippery floors; use nonskid floor wax
Sliding throw rugs	Replace sliding area rugs with nonskid rugs or put non-skid tape or pads beneath sliding rugs
Worn carpets	Repair or replace worn carpets
Upended/curled carpet edges	Tape down all carpet that can buckle or curl
Raised door sills	Remove raised doorsills or put carpet over them to make a smooth transition between rooms
Bathroom Problems	
Low toilet seat	Use raised toilet seat or install toilet safety frame

Inaccessible tub/shower stall	Install wall-mounted or tub-attached grab bar or shower chair/tub transfer bench
Slippery floor tiles	Apply non-skid strips/decals to bathroom tiled floors
Slippery tub/shower floor	Place non-skid rubber mat on tub floor
Stairway Problems	
Lack of handrails	Install well-anchored cylindrical handrails
Slippery steps	Apply non-skid treads to stairs
Steps in poor repair	Repair worn carpet on steps. Apply color contrasted non-skid tape for visibility
Furniture Problems	
Low chair seats	Replace low chairs with ones easy to get up from/sit down in
Armless chairs	Provide chairs with armrest support
Low/high bed	Replace existing mattress with one that is thicker to raise bed height or thinner to lower it
Storage Problems	
Shelves too low/high	Keep frequently used objects at waist level
Unstable chairs/step stools	Use reacher device to get objects

Lack of storage space   Install shelves and cupboards at accessible heights

What You Can Do

Modify your home as recommended above to reduce the probability of falls.

What Did You Say?

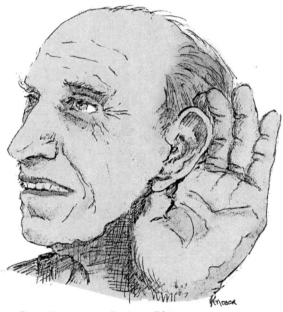

Ocular and Auditory
Seeing and Hearing

O is for

Ocular (Seeing) and Auditory (Hearing)

AGING AND VISION

Many older people have unrecognized eye problems that can be treated. Many have blurred vision. Some have **cataracts** where a film forms over the eye's lens. Others have **macular degeneration** where the central part of the retina weakens. Older people can lose depth perception. Some find distortion in how they perceive greens and blues.

Six Recommendations for Protecting Your Sight

1. If you find that your vision has changed, discuss it with your family doctor or an eye doctor (an ophthalmologist).

2. If you have a sudden onset of pain in your eye, go to the emergency room immediately. Such pain can be a sign of glaucoma (damage to the optic nerve) or possible blindness.

3. See an eye doctor regularly for checks on visual problems associated with aging. These include glaucoma, cataracts and macular degeneration.

4. Wear sunglasses when you are outside. They protect your eyes from the sun, overhanging branches and flying debris.

5. Always wear safety goggles when working with or near power tools.

6. Talk with your doctor about taking antioxidant vitamins to prevent macular degeneration.

SIGHT IS A PRECIOUS GIFT. CHERISH AND PROTECT IT.

AGING AND HEARING

Our senses—taste, touch, smell, sight and sound—connect us to the world around us. Hearing problems are the most frequent sensory impairment among older adults; 25 - 30% of Americans 65 and older cannot hear well. Hearing impairment is the most poorly recognized and under-corrected sensory impairment in our country. Only about 25% of people whom a hearing aid would help actually use one.

TYPES OF HEARING LOSS:

Presbycusis - This type of hearing loss occurs gradually as people age. In many instances, the patient can hear sounds but can't make words out of them. Certain consonants such as "s," "th," "h," and 'sh', are especially hard to differentiate. The patient might hear "thin" instead of "shin," "slap" instead of "tap."

Although hearing aids can restore useful hearing, some patients with presbycusis experience a dramatic increase in loudness when the sound source is amplified for them, and using a hearing aid can be painful.

Meniere's Disease - The symptoms of this disease are vertigo (the often extreme feeling that you are going to faint), tinnitus (ringing or buzzing in the ear) and hearing loss. Although medication can provide some relief, surgery is the only proven treatment for Meniere's Disease.

Acoustic Neuroma - This is a benign tumor that grows slowly on the vestibular nerve. It can bring on mild dizziness, tinnitus and hearing loss. The treatment is surgical removal of the tumor.

Conductive - Conductive hearing loss occurs when sound transmission to the inner ear is impaired. Sometimes, foreign bodies or skin tags blocking the ear are the culprits. About 30% of the people with conductive hearing loss have impacted cerumen (earwax) in their ears. Removing cerumen can improve conductive hearing loss. Have your doctor check your ears for cerumen or other blockages.

In extreme cases, hearing impairment can result in loneliness and isolation. Some hearing impaired-people have been mistakenly assumed to have a dementia disease such as

Alzheimer's. If you have any trouble hearing during a normal conversation, that's the first clue that you have a hearing problem. Talk with your doctor, who may send you to an audiologist, a specialist in hearing loss.

If you are close to someone who suffers from impaired hearing, you should understand that that person may be lip reading. DO NOT SPEAK LOUDER when you talk to a lip reading person. If you do, you will distort the shape of your lips, thus distorting the information you want to convey.

In addition to personal hearing aids, there are many useful listening assistive devices for telephones and televisions. Again, ask an audiologist for recommendations.

What You Can Do

Continue regular checkups with your family doctor. At the first sign of a vision or hearing problem, make an appointment with an ophthalmologist or an audiologist. Early detection and treatment of these problems will help you age successfully.

The Latest U.S. Health Epidemic

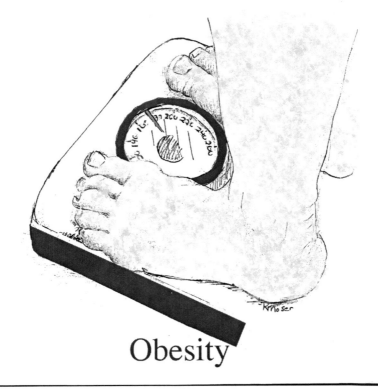

Obesity

O is for
Obesity and Diabetes Mellitus

An obesity epidemic is occurring in the United States, Canada and Great Britain. This epidemic includes youths whose changing lifestyles have them eating more and exercising less.

Although the terms *overweight* and *obesity* are often used interchangeably, they are defined differently. *Overweight* means weight above the normal range. *Obesity* means an excess of body fat and a weight more than 20% of ideal body weight. The Body Mass Index (BMI) measures excess weight. Your BMI is your weight in kilograms divided by your height in meters squared. Your physician can determine your BMI. For the white population, a BMI of 25-29.9 kilograms per meters squared is overweight. Obesity is a BMI of 30 or more. A BMI of 40 or more is severe obesity and the criterion used for surgical intervention.

Another excess weight measure is the Waist:Hip Ratio (WHR). This is determined by dividing waist circumference by hip circumference. Most people store body fat in two ways: around the waist (apple shaped) and around the hips (pear shaped). An apple shape is riskier for your health than a pear shape.

Type 2 Diabetes Mellitus and Obesity

Obese people are at high risk for developing Diabetes Mellitus Type 2.   Although some 20% of people aged 65-74 have this disease, about half of them may not know it.

Type 2 Diabetes Mellitus affects the arteries that carry our blood. When it affects small arteries, it can cause severe kidney and visual problems. When it affects large arteries, it can cause heart attacks and strokes. This is especially true for individuals who have also have high blood pressure (hypertension) and high cholesterol levels, other conditions associated with obesity.

Factors That Make People Especially Vulnerable to Type 2 Diabetes Mellitus:

Obesity	Age 45 or Older
Non-White Race	Family History of the Disease
High Blood Pressure	Impaired Glucose (Blood Sugar)
Tolerance	

What You Can Do

1. Have your doctor check you for diabetes. If you are diabetic, discuss treatment options with your doctor.

2. Consider walking one mile each day. Evidence suggests that this can prevent or delay the onset of Type 2 Diabetes Mellitus.

3. If you have high cholesterol and high triglyceride problems, ask your doctor about medications, especially if you are under 70. Obese people over 70 who smoke or have high blood pressure or diabetes should ask their doctors about medications that reduce high cholesterol and triglyceride levels. Medications known as *Statins* are effective and can be tailored to the individual patient's needs. *Statins* also seem to help prevent the onset of osteoporosis and Alzheimer's Disease.

4. Review the **N *is for Nutrition*** section.

5. Throw your TV remote clicker away. Some people who did that lost up to 15 pounds in a year thanks to the extra steps they took.

Cancer's Claws

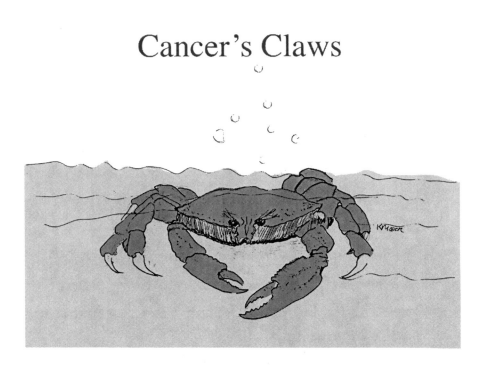

Neoplasm

N is for

Neoplasm (Cancers and Tumors)

A neoplasm is a new growth of tissue that the body does not need. Other words for neoplasm are cancers and tumors. A malignant (harm-causing) cancer can expand and invade other parts of the body. The spreading effect is called *metastasis*.

After heart disease, cancer is the second leading cause of death among adults. As we grow older, our chances of developing cancer increase dramatically. The most common cancers that cause death are:

LUNG CANCER

BREAST CANCER

PROSTATE CANCER

COLORECTAL CANCER

SCREENING FOR CANCER

This section of *BASIC PREVENTION* will focus on **Screening for Cancer**, testing that can identify cancer early enough so that it will respond to treatment. However, you should know recommendations about cancer screening can differ widely because more research needs to be done regarding what screenings are or are not effective. You should discuss the following recommendations about screenings for specific cancers with your doctor.

FOR WOMEN
BREAST CANCER

Forty-five percent of breast cancer cases occur in women over 65, and the percentage increases until about age 80. Breast cancer screening with clinical breast examination and mammography for women aged 40 is one of the best-established practices to identify and treat breast cancer early. Some authorities say screening every two years may be just as effective. I recommend continuing breast cancer screening at one- or two-year intervals for women over 70 who are in fairly good health and have a 5-10 year life expectancy. If you are a woman 40 or older, you should:

- Learn the technique for self-breast examination and perform it monthly.
- Schedule annual or biennial mammography with your doctor.
- Have your doctor perform a yearly breast examination on you. (Medicare and many other health care plans pay for every other year if normal or every year if there is a family history or an abnormal reading.)

CERVICAL CANCER

The neck of the uterus is called the cervix. The Pap smear, in which a small sample from the cervix is analyzed, is the test for cervical cancer. Cervical cancer is rare in older women; those with previously normal Pap smears rarely develop it. Older women who have not had previous Pap smears are more likely than younger women to have abnormal smears and cervical cancer. Here are my recommendations:

- If you have not had a pap smear in the past year, see your gynecologist or family doctor for one and follow up as recommended.
- Women with multiple sexual partners are at higher risk for cervical cancer.
- It is very prudent to see your gynecologist or family doctor every year for appropriate testing.

The incidence of cervical cancer appears to be related to the number of sexual partners a woman has. If you have had normal (negative) Pap smear results, remain in a monogamous relationship and are 65 or older, you probably do not need these tests any longer. But any abnormal vaginal discharge needs to be evaluated.

If, however, you acquire a new sexual partner later in life, ask your doctor if you should resume Pap smear screening.

OVARIAN CANCER

Ovarian cancers are very difficult to screen. The symptoms are increasing firmness/fullness in the lower abdomen. There is no evidence that any screening method- these include pelvic examination, ultrasound and serum tumor markers- improves the chances of successful treatment of an ovarian cancer. Nevertheless, I recommend women, regardless of age, undergo an annual pelvic examination.

FOR MEN

PROSTATE CANCER

Prostate cancer is second only to lung cancer as the leading cause of cancer deaths in men. The American Geriatric Society and the American Urological Association recommend:

- All men 50 and older have prostate cancer screening with a digital rectal examination and prostate antigen testing annually. This annual screening should continue as long as the individual has a ten-year life expectancy (on average between 70 - 75 years).
- Men who are at high risk due to a strong family history of prostate cancer begin these screenings at age 40.

But note, there is some disagreement regarding these recommendations. Other authorities question the value of routine prostate cancer screenings, saying the potential benefits in life extension are outweighed by the potentially harmful side effects: urinary incontinence, infection, impotence and rarely, but possibly, death.

I recommend:

- Healthy men under age 65 should talk with their doctors about the potential benefits and risks of prostate cancer screening.
- Screening is inappropriate for men who are very frail or very old.

COLON CANCER

There is no clear consensus on screening for colorectal cancer. Although digital rectal examinations are not effective screenings, the Fecal Occult Blood Stool Test, which tests for blood in the stools, can detect both premalignant lesions and early malignancies. It is inexpensive, and many authorities recommend it annually or every two years for people 40 and older.

People with a family history of colon cancer in a first-degree relative (parent, aunt, uncle, sibling) are considered at high risk for developing colon cancer. For this group, The American Cancer Society recommends one of the following:

- A complete colon evaluation, either by colonoscopy or barium enema, every ten years.
- A flexible sigmoidoscopy every five years.

- A Fecal Occult Blood Test annually.

Also: report any rectal bleeding to your doctor immediately.

Note: Colorectal cancer screening is not appropriate for people who are extremely frail.

To help avoid colon cancer:
- Take an aspirin a day
- Eat more low-fat, high-fiber foods

LUNG CANCER

Unfortunately, no lung cancer screening, including an annual chest X-ray or sputum analysis, is effective. The strongest recommendation we can make is to urge all smokers to quit.

SKIN CANCER

Skin cancers are common and 85-90% of them are in exposed areas. Melanomas are malignant tumors on the skin. These are usually in unexposed areas and can be much more dangerous than other skin cancers. You and your doctor should be on the alert for skin lesions, especially those with malignant qualities.

People at high risk for skin cancers should be examined by skin cancer specialists annually.

What You Can Do

Ask your doctor to arrange the cancer screenings appropriate for you. If treatment is recommended, begin it immediately.

Common Problems
An Aching Back

Back pain is very common among older adults. It is one of the Geriatric Syndromes. Commonly under-recognized and under-treated, back pain often leads to a decline in how a person functions in life. It can impair the ability to get around and increase the risk of falling. It can cause depression. Back pain can reduce a person's interaction with his or her community and consequently lead to physical isolation. It is important that we review some of the more common causes of back pain in order to do what we can to avoid them and to seek medical attention when needed.

Your back is made up of bony building blocks called vertebrae. Each vertebra is cushioned from the vertebrae above and below by a gelatinous disk called the vertebral disc. The seven vertebrae in the neck are the cervical vertebrae. As we descend from the neck we encounter 12 more vertebrae known as the thoracic vertebrae, which traditionally give us an outward curving of the spine. Below the thoracic vertebrae are five lumbar vertebrae. Below the lumbar vertebrae is the bony structure known as the sacrum. On the back of each vertebrae there are thinner bony structures that create a canal known as the spinal canal. The main nerve trunk that descends from our brain passes through the spinal canal, and as the spinal nerve descends the spinal nerve branches off to the left and to the right in order to send nerve impulses to and from the various organ structures and muscles of the body.

Your rib cage is made up of 12 ribs on each side of the body. Each of these is connected to the thoracic vertebrae. Large muscles known as the paraspinal muscle run along the length of the vertebrae. Muscles also connect each rib to another in order to flex and extend our backs and to assist in the expansion and contraction of our chest in the act of breathing. This basic description of our back will give you an understanding of the various causes of back pain.

There are many causes of back pain and more than one can exist at the same time. Therefore, it is important to pay attention to how back pain presents itself so as to sort out its cause or causes. The onset of back pain can be sudden or chronic. Its course can improve or worsen. It may be made worse with motion or it may be relieved with bed rest. The quality of the pain is important. It may be sharp, it may be dull, it may radiate to other parts of the body. For example, sciatic nerve pain may be a pulsating toothache-like pain that shoots down an entire leg into a foot. The cause of this pain is compression of nerves that come off the spinal cord at the level of the lumbar vertebrae.

If you have back pain, tell your physician what gives you relief: Heat? Ice? Change in position (lying, sitting, standing)? Tell your physician what medications provide you with some relief of your back pain such as Tylenol and aspirin-like compounds. Your physician will perform a neurological examination in order to determine sensory and motor functioning. He or she should palpate your back (examine by touch) and locate the tender points.

Back pain accompanied by symptoms of fever, weight loss and night sweats suggests a systemic cause: a tumor, infection, osteoarthritis, or referred pain from one of your body's organs such as the gallbladder or kidney.

Your pain may have different characteristics. The pain may be progressive and persistent and may not be affected by change in body position. On the other hand, back pain caused by a collapsed vertebrae due to osteoporosis is characterized by acute and sudden onset and may be relieved by lying flat.

Traumatic causes of back pain include motor vehicle accidents. A fractured rib can cause intense back pain.

There are two types of non-systemic causes of back pain. The first type is neurogenic and results from a herniated disk of the spine. The pain is sudden at onset and worsens with motion. This type of pain usually resolves with conservative treatment such as physical therapy, the application of heat and ice, and mild pain relievers. This type of pain can recur. The cause of the pain is due to the compress of nerves that come off the spinal cord through the vertebrae. Your physician will be able to determine what nerve roots are involved by the history of the onset and location of your pain.

The second non-systemic cause is spinal stenosis, which occurs when the canal that houses the spinal cord becomes narrow through changes of osteoarthritis and bone loss due to osteoporosis, or thinning of your bones. A typical symptom is a progressive subtle weakness that is usually worse with walking, and a pain generally relieved by flexing forward.

Other causes of back pain are mechanical. Muscle strain, for example, is acute in onset, localized and self-limiting. Other causes of pain are caused by degeneration such as occurs in osteoarthritis. The type of pain associated with osteoarthritis is acute in its onset, made worse with motion and generally recurs.

Your physician may use tests to help diagnose your back pain. X-rays of your spine will help confirm the diagnosis of osteoarthritis. An MRI scan will help determine some of the systemic causes of pain and will also help to identify disorders such as ruptured disks. In the physical examination, your physician will note leg length differences and other neurological abnormalities.

The treatment of back pain is generally conservative at first with the use of Tylenol, aspirin and non-steroidal anti-inflammatory agents. If necessary, muscle relaxers are added for paraspinal muscle spasms. The application of heat and ice are also a first line treatment. Physical therapy and massage are beneficial, as are brace supports if warranted. Your physician may refer you to either a neurosurgeon or orthopedic surgeon if severe symptoms persist beyond a reasonable period of time.

PREVENTION: A great deal of back pain can be avoided. Weight control and physical exercise are critical. Strengthening abdominal muscles is essential. Maintaining erect posture and getting into the routine of total body stretching exercises can help you avoid back pain. The intake of vitamin D can go a long way in preserving your muscle function. Screening for and treatment of osteoporosis can help prevent osteoporotic fractures of your spine. Brisk walking will promote bone growth. Bending at the knees rather than the hip can prevent back injury. Wearing the appropriate footgear is essential. Engage in balance exercise such as Tai-Chi. Practice fall prevention by inspecting your environment, maintaining your flexibility and paying attention to your eyes.

To summarize: Back pain is no fun. There are many different causes, some more worrisome than others. Do not delay seeing your physician. Get an appropriate diagnosis. Take charge. Take care of your back.

Chronic Pain

Pain is a very common geriatric syndrome. Chronic pain is the third most common cause that keeps people from enjoying life. Most of us have experienced acute pain at one time or another in our lives. Acute pain only lasts from hours to weeks. Remember when you had a toothache, stubbed your toe, or broke your arm? Those are examples of acute, short-term pain.

Many people suffer from chronic pain: pain that lasts longer than three weeks. The pain associated with arthritis is one example of chronic pain. Pain is a very important vital sign that tells us that something is wrong. A few individuals have a neurologic disorder that does not allow them to perceive pain. As a result, they tend to have shorter life spans.

Most of us will experience some type of pain as we go through our aging process. The intensity of pain may vary from slight to intolerable. Pain can have many different causes and types. I want you to be familiar with the different types of pain in order for you to seek proper pain relief help. Most types of chronic pain cannot be relieved totally. The goal of treatment should be to reduce the pain to a level at which you can function in performing life's daily chores.

Pain comes in various forms. One is called *nociceptive,* of which there are two types: *somatic* and *visceral.* The somatic type includes pain associated with surgery or injury to bones, joints and muscles. Movement intensifies this pain as does pressure applied to the injured area. Visceral pain is associated with inflamed or diseased organs, such as the brain (migraine headaches), an inflamed appendix or gall bladder and constipation. This type of pain is generally described as coming and going, cramping and often associated with bloating.

Another form of pain is called *neuropathic.* Caused by pinched nerves, this kind of pain, which usually runs along a sensory nerve, is often described as shooting, burning, stabbing or scalding. A light touch or mild pressure can intensify it. This kind of pain does not respond completely to opiate-based medicines. Other drugs such as Neurontin are often necessary.

Pain can have multiple factors that include:

- Physical pain
- Depression that can intensify pain
- Social isolation, often experienced by cancer patients
- Spiritual pain that comes from the question, "Why did this happen to me?"

It is important to differentiate what type of pain you're having, because the treatments for these pain syndromes differ. Make sure that you give your physician a very accurate description of your pain.

The World Health Organization recommends a stepladder approach to the treatment of chronic pain. For very mild pain acetaminophen (Tylenol), aspirin and anti-inflammatory drugs are the first choice of treatment. These agents can be used in combination with the application of heat and ice, massage and physical therapy. If the pain becomes moderate to severe, one can judiciously use short acting opiate-like compounds such as codeine or percocet. For very severe pain, longer acting morphine-like agents are available. These come in many forms and can be given orally, applied through the skin in a patch, or, if necessary for severe relentless pain, given through a pump system with a needle inserted just under the skin. These agents are generally effective, but all have side effects for which your physician can prescribe symptom management.

The details of all these different pain-relieving agents are too complex to include in this book. Much has been learned about the treatment and relief of pain through the Hospice and Palliative Care Programs. We have learned that neuropathic pain can sometimes be diminished with the use of medications that will block the perception of pain in the brain. Neurontin is a frequently used drug for this purpose.

There are a few key points that I want you to be aware of:

1. No one should suffer from extreme pain.
2. Physicians for the most part are not doing a great job of relieving pain.
3. There are specialists for pain management. You may have to be referred to one if you suffer from excruciating pain.
4. Many individuals shy away from taking opiate medications (morphine, methadone, fentanyl) for the fear of becoming addicted. Opiate types of medications are needed to relieve the pain associated with metastatic cancer. Hardly anyone develops an addiction to opiates. A person may develop tolerance; that is, over time one may need increasing doses of the medication, but this must not be confused with psychological dependency.
5. Not everyone responds the same way to opiate medication. It may take trial and error to find the one in which the patient can find pain relief, and at the same time, tolerate the side effects of the opiate medication. Physicians skilled in pain management and in Hospice and Palliative Care can help you find a balance between pain relief and side effects such as nausea, vomiting and confusion.
6. Patients in a terminal state and with severe pain can become confused when they live through past conflicts

as they go through the dying process. This confusion is different from the side effects of the opiate medications. Not all confusion is due to the medicine.

Finally, I repeat: No one should accept that he or she must live in severe chronic pain. The goals of pain therapy should be to maximize how a person can function and perform in order to complete things that he or she wants to do. I recommend that you discuss your physical and emotional concerns with your physician. You should communicate clearly your personal goals and wishes. You should expect that your personal wishes be honored. You should make clear the type of pain that you are experiencing and the amount of pain. You should review with your physician whether or not you're having any appetite loss or anxiety, incontinence of urine or bowel, and report issues of nausea and vomiting. Always report any symptoms of shortness of breath, any ulceration in your mouth or on your skin. Be mindful of any loss of your ability to bathe or dress yourself, toilet yourself, get out of bed and into a chair, and eat independently. This information is critical in order for your physician to be able to understand the severity of your pain and the impact of the pain is having on your life. Always remember that you and your physician must work as a team in order to optimize the strategies that will relieve you of your pain. Let me emphasize it once again: **no one should be left in pain.**

Constipation

Many older adults—36% of men and 21% of women—suffer from constipation. A glaring sign of constipation is that one out of four—25%—of older adults in developed nations use laxatives.

Causes of constipation include:

- Lack of water in the colon. For various reasons, older people drink less water
- Medications, including antacids, antidepressants, cold medicines, tranquilizers, cough syrups and many others
- Excessive use of laxatives

MANAGING CONSTIPATION

First, a physician or health care provider should review the constipated person's medications and modify them as necessary. Screening for serum potassium, calcium and magnesium is a must. The person should be evaluated for diabetes mellitus and an under active thyroid. Treating those underlying disorders or changing the medication may be the only treatment needed to stop the constipation.

Here is some advice on how to manage constipation:

- Use a bulk-forming agent such as **Metamucil** and increase fluid intake. Drink at least eight glasses of water or other liquids daily.
- **Sorbitol** is a fairly reliable laxative.
- Stool softeners have limited effectiveness.

Stimulant laxatives are effective sometimes but are subject to overuse. Use them only in the context of a program that calls for increased water intake and scheduled bathroom visits. Stimulant laxatives can harm the colon's ability to do its job. The more you take them, the worse you may become. This requires you to take more, creating a vicious cycle.

Avoid using *Mineral Oil;* it can have bad side effects.

Note that the hectic pace of our society contributes to constipation, especially among younger, active people. Drinking a cup of coffee and then taking a newspaper or good book to the bathroom may be all that's required.

CONSTIPATION REMEDY

Here's a recipe my patients find effective::

1 cup Apple Sauce

1 cup Unprocessed Bran

½ cup Prune Juice

Mix together in a Tupperware dish and refrigerate. Take two tablespoons with a glass of water at night. You may increase this to 4-5 tablespoons if needed. It can also be warmed before using.

Eat sensibly. (See **N** *is for Nutrition* in **BASIC PREVENTION**) and drink plenty of fluids. You will have good results.

Remember the old advice: *An apple a day keeps the doctor away.* That's a simple way of advising us to include roughage (fruits and vegetables) in our diets. Our country is rich in fruits and vegetables. Eating more of them will help lower the constipation rate.

Delirium

Delirium is the medical term for episodes of acute confusion. It is fairly common in older adults. Delirium has these characteristics:

- Delirium can come on quickly and last for hours or even days.
- Delirious people find it hard to shift attention and to concentrate on simple things like reading a newspaper or watching TV . Delirious people may be disoriented in time or in place. They may become agitated, paranoid (thinking that others want to harm them) and suffer hallucinations (seeing people or objects that are not really there).
- Delirious people's levels of consciousness can shift rapidly. They can go from being bright and alert to drowsy, stuporous, or even comatose. These shifts can reverse: a stuporous, delirious person can quickly become bright and alert.

Although people suffering from delirium are often mistakenly assumed to be demented, there are important, basic differences between delirium and dementia. Delirium comes on quickly and lasts for hours or days. Dementia develops more slowly and is incurable. Demented people's levels of consciousness don't shift; they are permanently confused.

The primary causes of delirium are old age and a preexisting dementing illness. As we age, our brains constantly lose cells that are not replaced, and the brain can be the organ least capable of withstanding psychologic stress such as infection. As a result, the brain may become confused and cause delirium even though the real disease is in another organ.

Disease, accidents, changes in environment and drug-related states may not appear in older people as they do in younger ones. A heart attack in an older person may be painless but cause confusion. Instead of the fever and rapid breathing typical of young pneumonia patients, older people with pneumonia may become delirious. Older people with appendicitis and urinary tract and other infections may not show the normal symptoms of fever and pain but rather become delirious.

Between 15 and 30% of older patients in hospitals become delirious during their stay. Between 30 and 50% of people who have hip or knee replacement surgery have delirium. Most of these recover from delirium quickly. Those who do not may be unable to return to a normal life and may require the services of a nursing home.

Delirium is a *medical emergency*. Medical staff must be on the lookout for it, identify its cause, and treat it promptly.

Treating Delirium

To treat delirium is to treat its cause(s). Among those causes are:

DRUGS. Drugs in general are probably the most common cause of delirium. Alcohol is a common cause. A drunken person can become delirious. But almost any drug can cause delirium, even an aspirin or an over-the-counter pain remedy such as Ibuprofen or Aleve. Over-the-counter cold remedies are common causes because of their effect on brain tissue.

We live in a drug-oriented society and we frequently look for remedies for insomnia, anxiety and pain. Drugs for these purposes frequently cause delirium, especially when the pain remedy includes opiates (morphine-like compounds).

DEPRESSION. Depression can be a chronic form of delirium. It is too often under recognized and under treated. (See the section on *Depression.*)

CHANGE IN ENVIRONMENT. Changes in environment (location) can trigger delirium, especially for older adults with poor hearing and vision. Many older adults find hospitals hostile environments and "strange places" where they become hypervigilant and very confused.

METABOLIC CAUSES. Metabolism is the way our bodies undergo chemical changes. Common metabolic causes of delirium include low or high blood sugar levels and low or high levels of serum sodium. People with kidney or liver failure may become delirious. These causes are frequently reversible and treatable.

ENDOCRINE SYSTEM ABNORMALITIES.

When the thyroid, adrenal and parathyroid glands produce abnormal levels of hormones, the patient may become chronically confused (and that confusion may be the only sign that something is wrong).

Other causes of delirium include brain traumas or stress, anemia and strokes.

In short, delirium can have many causes. Many who suffer from delirium have multiple causes going on at the same time. Consequently, evaluating and managing delirium are critical.

There are medications that make the patient comfortable while an evaluation takes place, but these do not treat the delirium. Most people recover from delirium, but the length of recovery can vary greatly. Family and caregivers can play a great role in the management and treatment of delirious patients. The presence of someone close—even a few favorite items brought from home—at the hospital can help reorient a confused patient. The presence of a loved one is often worth a pound of medications.

If someone close to you becomes acutely confused, arrange for medical attention *immediately*. Bring the person's medications and what you know of his/her medical history. Your knowledge of when the onset occurred and other information will help the physician identify the delirium's probable cause.

A well-informed caregiver or family member is essential to the treatment of a delirious patient. Consider yourself part of the medical team. Ask the physicians and nurses questions about the patient's work up and prognosis. Your presence and input are extremely valuable, and you should be informed and updated on the patient's progress.

And finally, if you are living with someone who has dementia, Alzheimer's, for instance, any sudden worsening of his/her mood is probably delirium. If this happens, seek medical attention immediately.

Dementia: Alzheimer's Disease and Vascular Dementia

Dementia is the deterioration of the brain's ability to function normally in at least three of these areas: memory, cognitive skills, speech and language, visual/spatial skills and behavior. It is most common among the older population.

I'm going to give you a general background on dementia and tell you what dementia patients may experience and how they can be helped.

At the outset, you should know that occasional lapses in memory are to be expected as we grow older. If you're 70 or older and temporarily forget something that happened last week or last month, that's normal. That's not proof of dementia. Dementia is characterized by loss of mental abilities to the extent that the patient cannot function adequately in social and work situations.

Another thing to remember is that many of us may experience delirium at one time or another: during a high fever, after surgery, after excessive use of alcohol and/or drugs, etc. Delirium is acute and short term. It comes on without warning, reaches its peak immediately and is usually reversible and short term.

Dementia is different. It comes on slowly but to date is irreversible. Although there are ways to help patients maintain some degree of an acceptable quality of life, there is no cure.

TYPES

Although there may be as many as 70-80 types of dementia, the most frequent forms are:

Alzheimer's Disease, named for the German Physician who identified it in 1906, is by far the most common type of dementia, accounting for about 70% of the cases in the United States. This illness comes on gradually and damages brain cells one by one, reducing the brain's ability to function normally. As time passes and more cells are destroyed, the patient's mental abilities decrease.

Vascular Dementia, including *Multi-Infarct Dementia.* Here, the brain cells don't get the needed amount of blood. Small strokes (infarcts) damage small areas of the brain. As in Alzheimer's Disease, vascular dementia comes on gradually but, over time, reduces the patient's mental abilities severely. About 10% of dementia cases in the US are vascular. Another 15% are combinations of Alzheimer's and vascular.

SYMPTOMS

Dementia is a degenerative disease. It comes on gradually and may be barely noticeable in its early stage. Failing memory is among the first signs. Patients may forget what they did a few days ago and have difficulty in recalling names and other common information.

Every patient with dementia is different. We can't predict when deteriorating changes will occur, but we know they will. As time passes, patients find it harder to remember and to think. They find it harder to read, write and to make decisions.

As more time passes, patients may have trouble with shopping, handling money and cooking. Eventually, they may need help with such basic activities as washing, dressing, and eating.

TREATMENT

Although we still have no cure for dementia, we should follow these steps in dealing with people who have or whom we think may have dementia:

1. Review the patient's medical history and give a physical examination that includes a Computed Tomography (CT) of brain (unenhanced) and a mini-mental state (M.M.S.) exam.
2. Rule out causes of delirium.
3. Non-Pharmacological Interventions:
   - adjustment of environment
   - caregiver assistance

- evaluation of basic needs

4. Pharmacological Interventions:
  - low dose antipsychotics
  - low dose antidepressants
  - low dose antianxiety

5. Education of Caregivers/Families
  - links to community resources
  - support groups
  - counseling

And finally, remember that in dementia, as in many other geriatric-related illnesses, there is usually more than one patient. In addition to the principal patients, husbands and wives, sons and daughters, brothers and sisters, close friends, doctors, nurses and social workers bear, to varying degrees, the stress of dealing with dementia. Close family members will have to deal with very difficult questions. Can we continue to care for him/her at home? What help is available if we do? If we decide to place him/her in an assisted living setting, how do we choose one? What will the costs be?

Community resources include the Area Agencies on Aging, Alzheimer support groups and Alzheimer chat rooms and bulletin boards on the Internet.

Dementia places heavy burdens on the patients and on the people close to them. Until we find a cure, the healthiest response is to understand what dementia is and does and to make its victims as psychologically and socially comfortable as we can. Those who love and care for patients with dementia should not let the shadow of dementia darken their own lives to the extent that they lose the ability to enjoy the many pleasurable things, people, places, events around them.

Depression

Depression is one of the most common and weakening illnesses. It ranks with cognitive impairment, incontinence, and falls as one of the leading causes of functional disability.

MAJOR DEPRESSION is a condition that lasts for at least two weeks during which the patient is either in a depressed mood or is unable to experience pleasure. It is marked by at least five of these symptoms:

- Depressed mood most of the day, nearly every day
- Markedly diminished interest or pleasure in most activities for most of the day
- Significant weight loss or gain; appetite disturbance
- Insomnia or excessive sleeping
- Extreme restlessness or extreme lethargy
- Inappropriate feelings of guilt or worthlessness
- Diminished ability to think or concentrate; indecisiveness
- Recurrent thoughts of death, including suicide

DYSTHYMIA, by contrast, is a milder depressive disorder that affects at least 3% of the population. It is also marked by reduced ability to function effectively and a depressed mood. Less severe than major depression, dysthymia is present more than half the time over a two-year period. It is marked by at least two of these chronic symptoms:

- Appetite disturbances
- Insomnia or excessive sleeping
- Decreased energy or fatigue
- Low self-esteem
- Decreased ability to concentrate; difficulty in making decisions
- Feelings of hopelessness

Depression affects people of all ages, ethnic backgrounds and socio/economic status. The lifetime risk of having a depressive disorder is 10% to 25% for women and 5% to 12% for men. Because of the increasing awareness of depression worldwide, especially among the elderly, Primary Care Physicians (PCP's) can expect to see and screen increasing numbers of people with this condition.

DIAGNOSING DEPRESSION

Signs of depression are not always apparent in older adults, who can suffer from a condition called "masked depression." Earlier generations did not talk about their feelings. They thought going to a psychiatrist might label them as "crazy." Sometimes they express their internal feelings through physical complaints. I call these patients "organ grinders" because they will complain about almost every organ in the body, saying they have headaches, backaches, stomachaches, itching tongues, etc. These physical complaints are masking their real illness: depression. Family members and medical personnel must be sensitive to symptoms of masked depression.

Masked depression also occurs with other real illnesses: heart disease, diabetes, asthma, stroke and other conditions that cause chronic pain. Though it may be masked in certain patients, depression is very real and should be treated.

Depression is often a result of some common medical conditions that include:

- An underactive thyroid gland
- An overactive thyroid gland
- An overactive parathyroid gland

In these instances, when we treat the glandular condition, we remove the depression.

Finally, patients diagnosed with cancer often become depressed. With pancreatic cancer, however, depression may be the *only* symptom. As with the glandular conditions, treating the pancreatic cancer can remove the depression.

TREATING DEPRESSION

The three types of treatment for depression are: medication, psychotherapy and electroconvulsive therapy.

Treatments for depression are both safe and effective. The most common, by far, is medication accompanied by some brief counseling (psychotherapy). Patients who do not respond to medication and psychotherapy treatment may receive electroshock therapy, a completely safe procedure that can be delivered on an outpatient basis.

Doctors now have a broad range of safe and effective medications that treat depression. Since every anti-depressant medicine has one or more side effects, doctors choose the medicine with side effects that will benefit the patient. For a depressed patient who sleeps excessively, a doctor will describe an anti-depressant with a side effect that reduces the desire for sleep. For a depressed patient with insomnia, a doctor will choose an anti-depressant with a side effect that induces sleep. A depressed patient with urinary incontinence may take an anti-depressant with a side effect that will relieve the bladder problem.

Depression is a serious illness; don't take it lightly. There is a great deal of misunderstanding about depression and its treatment and about psychiatry in general. Many older adults are reluctant to admit they are depressed. Treatment can allow a depressed person to live a physically, psychological, socially and spiritually satisfying life.

WARNING: Self-medication for depression with herbal remedies is NOT recommended.

A QUICK SCREEN FOR DEPRESSION

Here is a quick screen for someone you might consider depressed. Ask these two questions:

During the past month, have you often had little interest or pleasure in doing things?

Have you felt down, depressed or hopeless?

If the answer to both questions is NO, the screen is negative.

If the answer to either question is YES, the person should have an in-depth depression evaluation by a primary care physician or psychiatrist.

IN-DEPTH   DEPRESSION   EVALUATION
QUESTION A

Over the past two weeks, how often have you been bothered by these problems?

Circle the appropriate response. (0 = not at all; 1 = several days; 2 = more than half the time; 3 = nearly every day.)

1 Little interest or pleasure in doing   0 1 2 3
things

2 Feeling down, depressed, or hopeless   0 1 2 3

3 Trouble falling asleep, staying asleep, 0 1 2 3
or sleeping too much

4 Feeling tired or having little energy   0 1 2 3

5 Poor appetite or overeating.   0 1 2 3

6 Feeling bad about yourself, thinking   0 1 2 3
that you are a failure or that you have
let your family down

7. Trouble concentrating on things like   0 1 2 3
reading the newspaper or watching
television

8. Moving or speaking so slowly that   0 1 2 3
other people notice
or being especially fidgety and restless

9 Thinking you would be better off   0 1 2 3
dead or wanting to hurt
yourself in some way

SCORING QUESTION A

Add up your scores.

Less than 4:   The patient may or may not be
depressed.

5 – 14: Significant depression. A doctor should decide on treatment based on the duration of the symptoms and the extent of functional impairment.

15 or more: Warrants treatment using anti-depressant medicines or psychotherapy or a combination of both.

QUESTION B

If you checked off any problems on this questionnaire, how difficult have these problems made it for you to do your work, take care of things at home or get along with other people?

Not difficult at all___   Somewhat difficult___   Very difficult___   Extremely difficult___

SCORING QUESTION B

The last two responses for this question suggest that the patient's functionality is impaired. This question is useful in both identifying depression and monitoring a patient's response over time to treatment.

Dizziness

Many older adults complain about dizziness. You should know two major things about dizziness: First, it's a common problem that if left unrecognized and untreated can result in depression, falls and fractured bones, limited mobility and isolation. Second, although there are various causes of dizziness, most people who suffer from them can be cured or taught techniques to prevent falls and injuries.

FOUR KINDS OF DIZZINESS

Doctors should not define dizziness for their patients. Instead, they should have patients describe their symptoms in their own words. We recognize four distinct kinds of dizziness that have different causes and require different treatments. Patients' descriptions of their symptoms guide the physician to the real causes and proper treatments. A wrong treatment can cause great harm.

Type 1: True Vertigo. The symptom here is that the room is spinning around the patient or the patient is spinning around the room. Patients can also have fairly severe nausea and vomiting. The most common cause of true vertigo is *Acute Labyrithitis,* a disorder that blocks the ear's semicircular canal, where our sense of space—our awareness of whether we are standing or sitting, turning right or turning left, etc.—is lodged. When the semicircular canal is blocked, our sense of where we are in space gets scrambled. *Acute Labyrinthitis* often results from an infection related to flu season or allergies. The uncomfortable symptoms may last from 4-6 weeks but generally resolve on their own. Fluids, rest, reassurances and, possibly, anti-nausea medications are the only remedies required.

But *Acute Labyrinthitis* may also be caused by an *endolith*, a small calcium deposit that forms in the semicircular canal and can cause chronic labyrinthitis. Fortunately, this condition occurs infrequently. Unfortunately, when it does occur it may take a long time to resolve or may never resolve. Patients with chronic labyrinthitis should be treated by a physician or neurologist. A neurologist or physical therapist can prescribe exercises that greatly relieve chronic labyrinthitis symptoms.

Type 2: Disequilibrium. Here, the symptom is the discomfort of not knowing where the ground is under one's feet. It's the same feeling people may get when they are in a rapidly descending elevator or when getting out of a chair or bed. One cause is that the aging process can keep our blood vessels from contracting as quickly as they did when we were younger. The result is that when older people go from sitting or lying to standing, it takes longer for their blood to flow to the center of balance in the brain. After a moment or two, the blood gets there and the symptoms abate. Some people say that if they stand suddenly it takes them a few seconds to get their "land legs."

Heart conditions such as valvular heart disease and irregular heartbeat rhythms can also result in disequilibrium. The symptoms can be controlled and falls avoided by simply understanding what's happening and taking the time to get up slowly and holding on to something fixed and steady—a wall, a table—until the symptoms stop.

People with osteoarthritis or diabetes, and especially those with severe arthritis of the neck, may also have disequilibrium. They may find that in walking to the bathroom at night, or even walking on pavement or in the garden during the day—they don't feel secure. Using a cane, which is really an extension of one's finger, will tell them where the ground under their feet is. Holding onto a wall or a piece of furniture gives the same kind of security.

Type 3: Vertebrobasilar Artery Insufficiency. The symptom is dizziness when you bend your head back or bend it forward. This happens when two small arteries in your neck kink (like a garden hose can kink) and stop blood from flowing into your brain's balance center. The treatment is simple: avoid bending your head forward or backward quickly. Some patients wear a soft collar around their necks as a reminder not to bend quickly. People with this type of dizziness can have unpleasant experiences when they bend down to tie a shoe or check the garbage disposal under the sink. But it's a condition you can learn to live with safely.

Type 4: Depression. This can be a Catch 22 situation. People who fall because of dizziness develop a fear of falling. They will often isolate themselves to safe environments and feel their world has become restricted. They may become depressed, a condition treated with antidepressant medicines. BUT, anti-depressant medicines that cause a sudden drop in blood pressure can stop blood from flowing to the brain's balance center and thus cause more dizziness! The patient's doctor should check to make sure that a medication and its dose to cure the fear of dizziness is not contributing to the problem.

Incontinence

In recent years, advertising for adult bladder protection products has pulled incontinence out of a quiet background and into the public spotlight – right where it should be. The condition is so common that to keep it hidden from view would be discounting the large percentage of the older population who experience it. In fact, about one-third of women and one-fifth of men in retirement communities live with incontinence. More than half (53%) of very frail older people, especially those with dementia, suffer from it.

The effects of urinary incontinence are devastating. It is a leading cause for admissions to nursing homes as caregivers become exhausted from cleaning soiled bed clothes and clothing. People become depressed as they find themselves restricted to their homes for fear of becoming embarrassed in public. At worst, older adults may slip in a pool of their urine, fall down and fracture a hip or a leg, a situation that will compound their incontinence problems.

The economic loss of managing urinary incontinence and its complications is *enormous*, with estimates of more than $10 billion annually in the United States alone. Clearly, it is not a condition that affects a select few.

In brief, a person who urinates involuntarily because he/she can't control the bladder is said to be incontinent. We are going to look at the condition of *severe urinary incontinence*, which is the inability to control the bladder one or more times a week.

Let's start at the beginning. As children, we naturally become *continent* able to control our urination. Our kidneys process the liquids from our diet into urine to be stored in our bladders. Just like air fills a balloon, urine fills our bladders. When the bladder is reasonably full, it sends a signal to the brain that says it's time to empty the bladder. Normally, we get these signals in plenty of time to find a bathroom. When we are there, the brain tells the bladder to open and empty the urine. When we are finished, the brain tells the bladder to close and prepare to store the new urine the kidneys will produce over the next few hours. Throughout most of our lives, this basic signaling system between the bladder and the brain keeps us continent with almost no additional effort on our part.

But like every body system, aging means changing. The chief reason for severe urinary incontinence among people 70 and older is the breakdown of the brain to bladder signaling system. We'll review some of the causes and outcomes in a moment.

Before we look at the types and degrees of incontinence, you should know this *very important and optimistic fact:* **At** least 70% of the people who suffer from severe urinary incontinence can be restored to normal urination patterns or at least have their incontinence diminished to a level that no longer interferes with their social and personal lives.

CAUSES OF SEVERE URINARY INCONTINENCE

First, what brings on severe urinary incontinence? Those normal aging changes can affect a person's urination. Some specific factors that disrupt the brain to bladder signaling system include:

- **Damage:** Brain damage from a stroke or from the effects of Alzheimer's Disease
- **Disruptions:** Accidents, strokes, infections, tumors, and other processes that disrupt the spinal cord connection that links the brain and bladder
- **Disease:** Defects in the bladder itself resulting from long-standing diabetes or multiple sclerosis
- **Drugs:** Certain medications that alter the signaling system or cause the bladder muscle to be constantly relaxed and enlarge the bladder

While these factors are certainly serious and can require professional medical attention, other causes of severe urinary incontinence can be easily reversed. These "transient causes" include:

- **Inability to get to a bathroom in time.** A restrictive problem, it may be because the patient is in a cast, confined to bed rest, or unable to move quickly enough because of arthritis
- **Confusion** resulting from an illness that disturbs the brain
- Temporary bladder infections
- **Kidney stones** that have found their way into the bladder
- **Prostate enlargement** in men
- **Stool impaction** that blocks urine from flowing out of the bladder
- **Medications,** including water pills and certain heart medications that cause large amounts of urine to accumulate in the bladder and result in frequent urination
- **Excessive use of caffeine** in coffee, tea, and hot chocolate that causes the bladder to contract constantly
- **Uncontrolled diabetes** that causes the kidneys to try to rid the body of excessive sugar by voiding a lot of fluid. This leads to frequent urination and, sometimes, to urinary incontinence

CONTROLLING SEVERE URINARY INCONTINENCE

As you can see, many of the causes of this condition can be addressed and corrected with some logical steps. So let's review some things you can do that may prevent or delay urinary incontinence.

Check Your Prescriptions: Ask your doctor how your medications might affect your bladder.

Check Your Eyes: Ensure good vision with updated eyeglass lenses and keep good lighting between the bedroom and bathroom. It is quite common for older adults to urinate three to four times during a sleep cycle, so keep the path visible and clear. Poor vision can keep a sleepy person from finding the bathroom.

Stay Fit: Exercise sensibly so your muscles have the strength to get you on and off the toilet.

Stay Away From Coffee: Limit the use of caffeinated beverages; they can increase the need to urinate. In men, caffeine can also have a negative effect on the prostate.

Say No to Nightcaps: Avoid excessive use of alcohol.

Monitor Other Health Systems: Control your blood pressure.

Use the Facilities Often: Take time out to go to the bathroom. "Holding it" can weaken the muscles in your bladder.

All too frequently, the medical profession treats urinary incontinence as a *diagnosis*, that is, as the central problem rather than as a *symptom* of one or more treatable conditions. If you or a loved one suffer from urinary incontinence, don't allow your physician to be complacent about it. Get the advice of a team of specialists who can evaluate the problem from the different aspects we've reviewed.

KINDS OF URINARY INCONTINENCE

Finally, be aware of some forms of urinary incontinence that require medical or pharmacological intervention even if such intervention cannot cure the problem. These are:

Urge Incontinence: Some patients suddenly feel that they must urinate and immediately release a large amount of urine before they can get to a bathroom. This condition frequently occurs in people who have had strokes that cause the brain to lose control over the signaling system to the bladder. People with dementia may also have this condition.

Valve Dysfunction: In older women, the muscles that hold the bladder and vagina in place may become weakened. As a result, the internal sphincter the valve that opens and closes the bladder—is displaced and functions improperly. When a simple incident such as coughing, sneezing, jumping or getting out of a chair puts pressure on the abdomen, that pressure can force urine out of the bladder through the faulty valve.

Atrophic Vaginitis: The loss of estrogen on the lining of the vagina can frequently make older women feel they must urinate. Topical therapy with estrogen may be appropriate to treat this condition. However, there are significant risks related to estrogen, including cancer. Consult your physician to determine the right strategy for you.

Overflow Incontinence: Prostate problems in men and vaginal disturbances in women can result in difficulty in emptying the bladder, a condition called *overflow incontinence*.

Remember, there are many kinds of urinary incontinence and just as many medical treatments for it. Most importantly, **do not** accept urinary incontinence as a natural part of old age. Talk with your family physician or a urologist or, for women, a gynecologist. Timely and appropriate treatment for incontinence will prevent further decline and keep you right where you should be – in the public spotlight.

WHAT YOU SHOULD LOOK FOR IN A PHYSICIAN

You will recall that at the end of each of these chapters I have recommended that you discuss all recommendations with your personal physician. I cannot emphasize enough that you and your physician make up a team that will become a good team. I have challenged you to be proactive about your care and take the initiative to be responsible on your journey to successful aging. You cannot do this without your personal physician, nurse practitioner or physician's assistant. In order to complete these recommendations for Basic Prevention you need to be working with a "good" practitioner. As a conclusion to this book, I offer you my perspective on what makes up a good physician or practitioner.

When I graduated from medical school, I walked across the stage and was handed a diploma. This diploma was a ticket to the "doctor guild."

This diploma, however, did not imply that I was a good doctor. To become a good doctor requires time and experience. Here are the traits that I perceive to be essential to be a "good" doctor. Look for these when you must choose a new physician or healthcare provider and reflect to see if these exist in your current provider.

1. Your healthcare provider must be as scientifically knowledgeable as possible. This is what you must demand of your physician. Check to see if your physician is a graduate of a qualified medical school and that he or she has received board certification in his field of study. Also, check to see if he or she has received additional training as a sub-specialist. Inquire how your physician is perceived by his or her colleagues on the medical staff of your hospital. And also inquire about his or her endeavors to keep current with continuous medical education. Being a good hand holder without true scientific knowledge is dangerous.

2. The second quality of a good physician is to be compassionate. Compassion is the ability to look into a patient's eyes and to listen to the patient's need to be listened to, communicated to and held in high regard as a person with integrity and self-worth. Ask yourself whether your doctor knows your personal belief system and values. Simply put, does he or she really care for you as a person?

3. The third quality of a good physician is a quality of goodness. This quality is generally the hardest to describe but easiest to recognize. Goodness are those small acts that are done behind the scenes to help make another's life less burdensome and more comfortable. You can get a sense of this through his or her handshake and greeting. Listen carefully; physical appearances may be deceiving but the human voice always reflects the speaker's true feelings.

4. The fourth quality of a good physician is the outward manifestation that he or she acknowledges that the energy that is required to be a healthcare provider comes from a source much greater than ourselves. The physician and healthcare provider are truly agents of a higher power. The role of a healthcare provider is very similar to the priest, rabbi, minister, and that is to provide guidance to other human beings on how to meet and transcend the challenges of life. It is also true that good physicians can cure sometimes, but care always.

I hope that you have enjoyed this straightforward approach to successful aging. Here's to your good health.

AND IN CONCLUSION...

Americans are living longer. In 2000, our average life expectancy was 75 (77 for women, 73 for men). <u>Basic Prevention</u> will help you lead a healthier as well as a longer life. The advice and recommendations I give in it come from more than 30 years of medical practice in treating older adults. Much of what I have written here reflects up-to-date medical practice. Some of it comes from observing thousands of patients. And some is plain old common sense. Put together, they add up to a guide to aging successfully.

When you follow the *What You Can Do...* recommendations, you are on the path that will help you to be "young old" and enjoying life, the path that can reduce the time, if any, when you may be "frail old" and dependent on others.

Although <u>Basic</u> <u>Prevention</u> often advises you to speak with your doctor, it really puts you in charge of your body and its health. Do you want to age successfully? Of course you do, and now you have a guide on how to do it. Taking charge of your health now can brighten your future years.

Printed in the United States
203344BV00004B/118-201/P